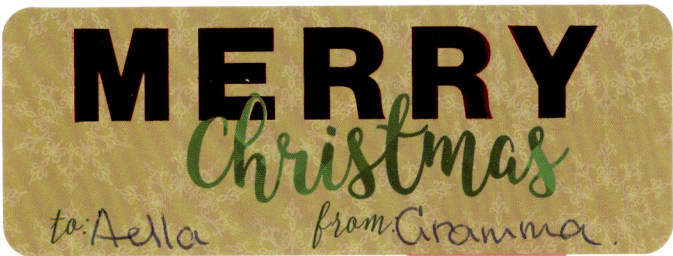

MERRY
Christmas

to: Aella   from: Gramma.

MW01609327

MY
FANCY
DRESS
BOOK

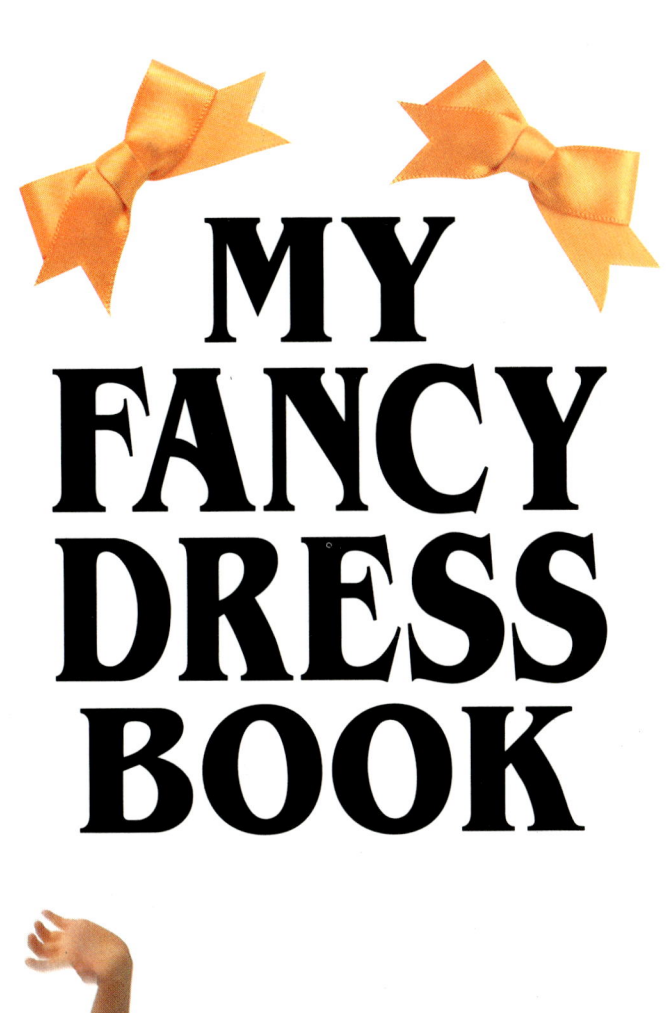

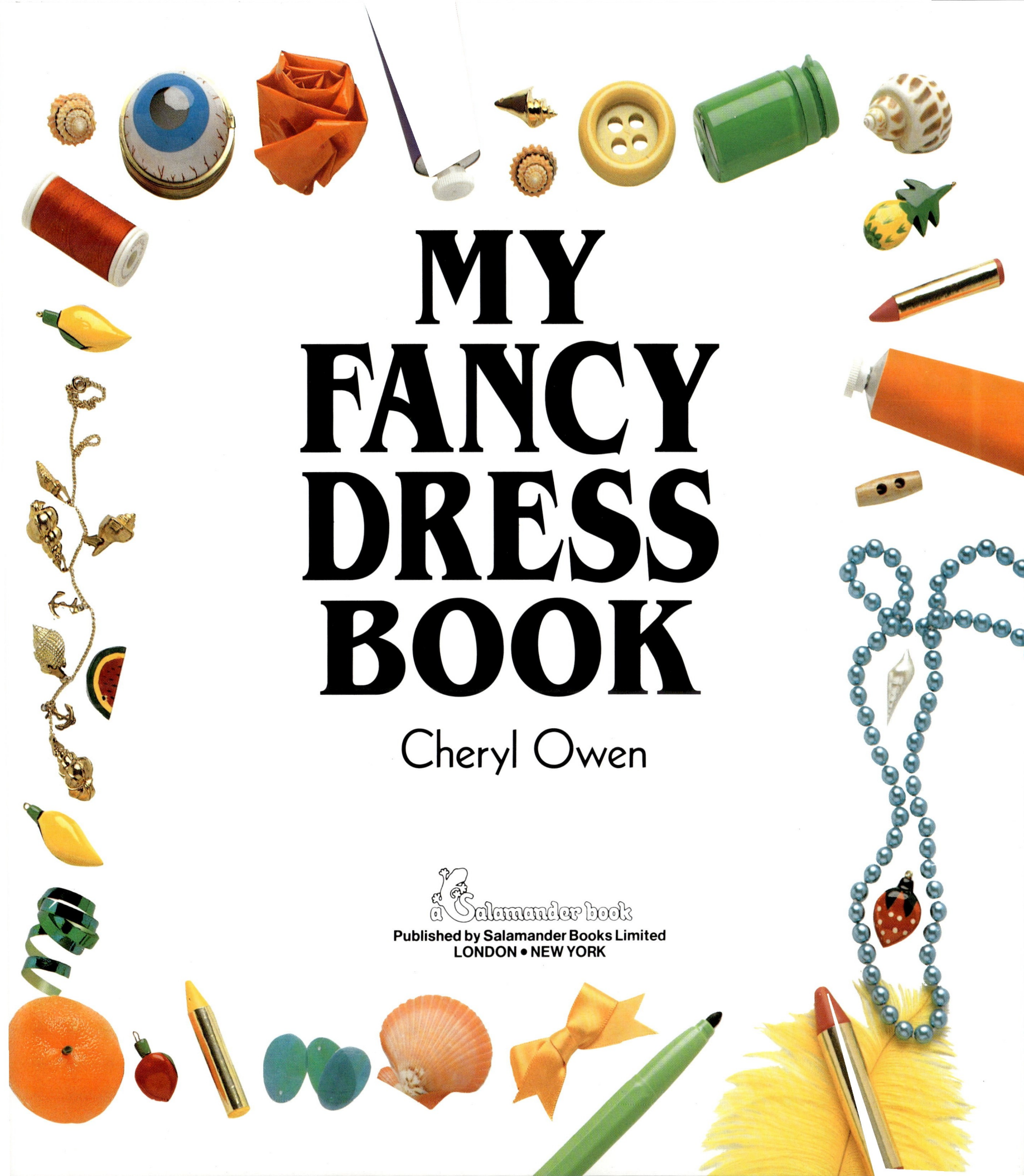

MY
FANCY
DRESS
BOOK

Cheryl Owen

a Salamander book

Published by Salamander Books Limited
LONDON • NEW YORK

A SALAMANDER BOOK

Published by Salamander Books Ltd.,
129-137 York Way,
London N7 9LG,
England.

ISBN 1 85600 035 4

Distributed by Hodder and Stoughton Services,
PO Box 6, Mill Road, Dunton Green,
Sevenoaks, Kent TN13 2XX.

1 3 5 7 9 8 6 4 2

CREDITS

Managing editor: Veronica Ross
Art director: Rachael Stone
Photographer: Jonathan Pollock
Assistant photographer: Peter Cassidy
Editor: Judith Casey
Illustrator: Teri Gower
Character illustrator: Jo Gapper
Diagram artist: Malcolm Porter
Typeset by: Quest Typesetting, London
Colour separation by: P & W Graphics, Pte., Singapore
Printed in Italy

The publishers would like to thank Kim Clarke,
educational craft and textiles consultant, for her help
and advice in compiling this book.

CONTENTS

INTRODUCTION

This colourful and imaginative book is packed with fancy dress costumes for you to make, each one with easy-to-follow instructions and colourful step-by-step pictures to help you. Get together with your friends and make the Strongman, Crazy Clown and Friendly Lion outfits for a circus theme party, or the Vampire, Wicked Witch and Little Devil for a spooky Hallowe'en party.

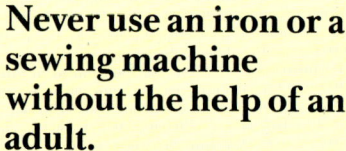

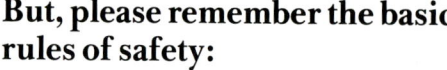

Never use an iron or a sewing machine without the help of an adult.

Be very careful when using sharp scissors, needles and pins.

BEFORE YOU BEGIN
- Do check with an adult before starting any projects; you might need some help.
- Read the instructions before you begin.
- Gather together all the items you need first.
- Cover the work surface with paper or an old cloth.
- Protect your clothes with an apron or wear very old clothes.

WHEN YOU HAVE FINISHED
- Tidy everything away. Store special pens, paints, glue, pins, needles and thread etc in old ice-cream containers or biscuit tins.
- Wash paintbrushes and remember to put the caps back on pens, paints and glue containers.

SAFETY FIRST!
Do use your common sense when using anything hot or sharp. You will be able to make most of the projects yourself, but sometimes you will need help from an adult. Look out for the SAFETY TIP. It appears on those projects where you will need to ask an adult for help.

But, please remember the basic rules of safety:
- Never leave scissors open or lying around where smaller children can reach them.
- Always stick needles and pins into a pin cushion or a scrap of cloth when you are not using them.
- Never use an iron, sharp scissors or a sewing machine without the help or supervision of an adult.

MATERIALS

Before you buy any materials to make a costume, check at home with an adult first as you may find some useful remnants of fabric and wool.

Ask your family and friends for old clothes that you could adapt for your outfits, and look in second-hand clothes shops and charity shops for hats, clothes, belts, shoes and other useful items. Start to collect buttons, beads, ribbon and braid that might come in useful for decorating your costumes.

Some items such as glitter paints, sticky-backed plastic and acrylic paints, will need to be bought from a craft supplier or a department store. When thick wire is needed, bonsai tree wire which can be bought at garden centres is best because it is very thick but can be bent into shape easily. Fuse wire can be used when fine wire is needed or use stub wire which is available at florists or craft shops.

EQUIPMENT

Every project will list all the things you need, and you will probably already have most of the equipment at home, but do check with an adult before taking anything. Make the paper patterns that are to be pinned on to fabric from old wallpaper, brown parcel paper or tracing paper, and use a tape measure and a ruler to check the measurements.

If you have a sewing basket at home, ask an adult if you can hunt through it for scissors, pins, needles and thread. Pinking shears are good for cutting fabric as they stop the material from fraying. A sewing machine is useful for stitching pieces of fabric together, but always ask an adult to help you use it. Store pencils, felt-tip pens, glue, paints and brushes in a special box.

USING PATTERNS

At the back of the book you will find the patterns you will need to make many of the costumes in the book. To find out how to copy a pattern follow the step-by-step instructions given for each project. Some of the patterns are shown as diagrams with measurements so that you can draw the correct size pattern piece on to paper. To find out how to do this follow the instructions for Making a Paper Pattern on page 8.

Once you have gained confidence making some of the costumes featured in this book, go on to adapt the ideas to create your own designs. If you enjoy drawing, try making up your own patterns and designs freehand.

GROWN-UPS TAKE NOTE

Every costume in *My Fancy Dress Book* has been designed with simplicity, yet effectiveness, in mind. However, some potentially dangerous items such as irons and sharp scissors are used for some projects. Your involvement will depend on the ability of the child, but we do recommend that you read through any project before it is undertaken.

Get everything ready before you start, and don't forget to tidy up afterwards!

Read the instructions carefully before you begin.

BASIC TECHNIQUES

All the costumes featured in *My Fancy Dress Book* are easy to make, but before you start we do recommend that you learn some simple dressmaking techniques. On these pages you will find easy-to-follow instructions and step-by-step drawings for all the basic techniques we have used in the book. When you need to use a basic technique, the instructions for the costume you are making will tell you to refer to these pages.

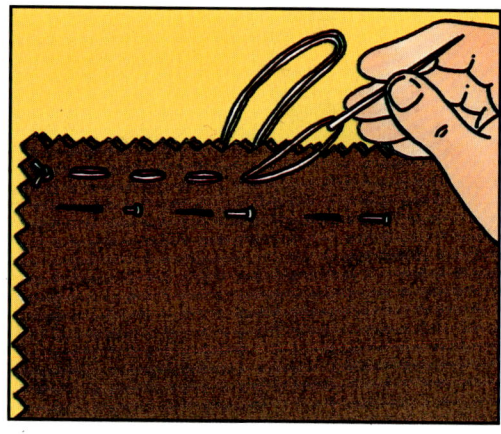

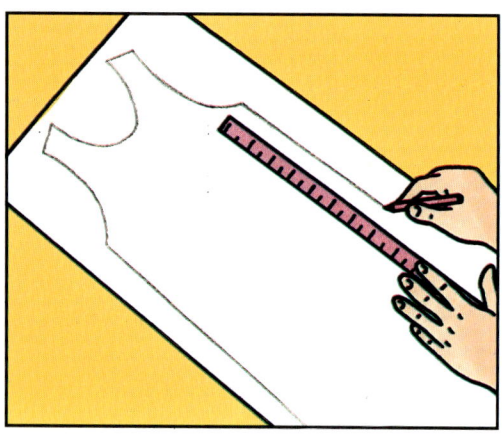

RUNNING STITCH

A simple running stitch is used to sew pieces of fabric together. Unless the instructions say otherwise, place costume pieces together with the right sides of the fabric facing. Pin the two pieces of fabric together, matching the raw edges.

Thread a needle with sewing thread and make a knot at the end. Now push the needle through the double layer of fabric to anchor the knot. Continue inserting the needle in and out of both layers of fabric, as shown, making the stitches about 5mm (¼in) apart and 1.5cm (⅝in) in from the edges. Knot the thread at the end of the seam.

MAKING A PAPER PATTERN

To make a full-size paper pattern from a diagram at the back of the book, you will first need to lay out a large sheet of wallpaper, brown paper or tracing paper on to a flat surface. You will need a pencil, ruler and a tape measure. Copy the diagram carefully on to the paper, carefully following the measurements and starting with the longest straight lines. Before you cut the pattern out, check all the measurements again and make sure that the curved shapes look the same as on the diagram. Now cut out the paper pattern.

CUTTING OUT FABRIC

Check the instructions to see how many pieces of fabric you need to cut out. If you need to cut two pattern pieces that are the same, fold the fabric in half and pin the paper pattern on to both layers of fabric. Now cut around the paper pattern to give two identical fabric shapes. If you need just one pattern piece, pin the paper pattern on to a single layer of fabric and cut out. Always cut out fur fabric pattern pieces one at a time and cut through the back of the fabric.

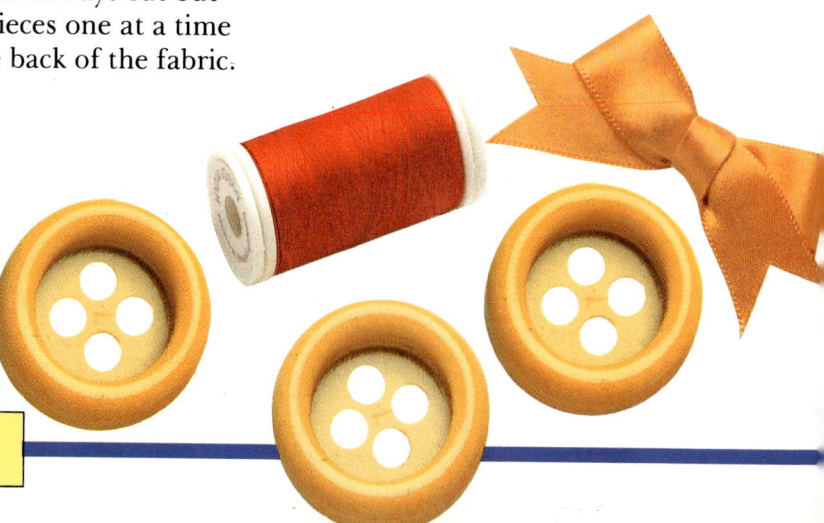

GATHERING FABRIC

1. To do this, thread a needle with sewing thread and make a knot at one end. Now sew a line of running stitch through the fabric, making the stitches about 13mm (½in) long and 1cm (⅜in) in from the edge. Do not make a knot when you have finished the stitching but leave the thread hanging. To gather up the fabric, gently pull the end of the thread and bunch up the fabric. If you are gathering up a long piece of fabric, divide the edge into quarters and start and finish the gathers at these points.

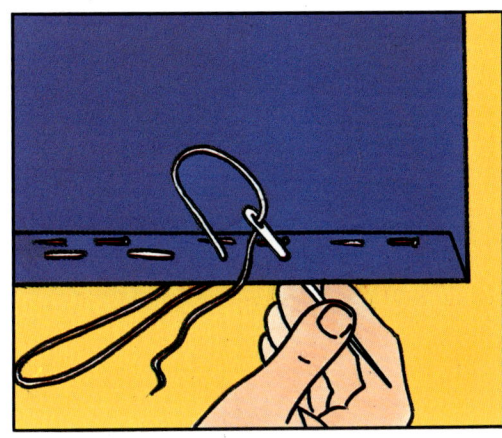

MAKING A HEM

To do this, turn under 1.5cm (⅝in) on the raw edge to the wrong side of the fabric and pin in position. Sew a neat line of running stitch through both layers of fabric. Now take out the pins.

MAKING A CHANNEL

1. To start, turn under 2cm (¾in) of fabric on the raw edge to the wrong side of the fabric. Sew a line of running stitch 1.5cm (⅝in) from the folded edge to make a channel. If you are making the artist's smock or the mermaid's bikini top and tail, leave a small gap between the beginning and the end of your line of stitches.

2. To attach the gathered piece of fabric to another piece of fabric, gently pull the gathers to fit and pin the frill in place. Stitch the two pieces of fabric together with small running stitches.

2. Now fix a safety pin to one end of the elastic, cord or ribbon and push the pin into the gap you left in the line of stitches. Feel for the pin through the fabric and ease it through the channel pushing back the fabric as you work. Pull the safety pin back out through the gap. If you are making the artist's smock or the mermaid's bikini top and tail, pin the ends of the elastic together. Try on the costume piece and adjust the elastic to fit. You may need to shorten the elastic if the costume piece is too big. Sew the ends of the elastic together.

PRESENT

For the ultimate gift – just present yourself! All you need for this idea is a large cardboard box and lots of giftwrap. The crêpe paper ribbon around the centre of the present helps to disguise any joins in the giftwrap and the large bow adds the finishing touch. Wear the box over a body stocking or a pair of tights and a T-shirt.

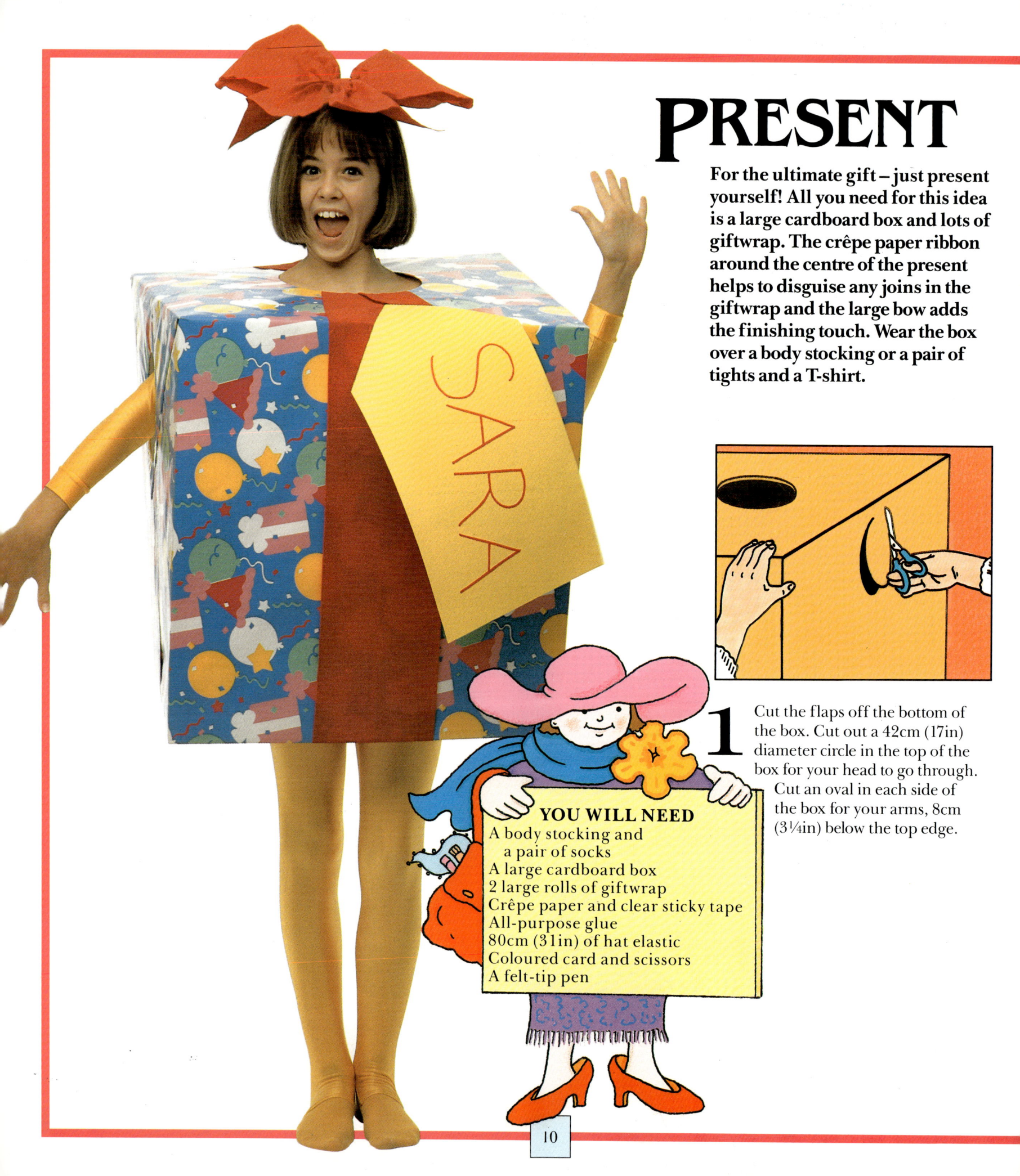

1 Cut the flaps off the bottom of the box. Cut out a 42cm (17in) diameter circle in the top of the box for your head to go through. Cut an oval in each side of the box for your arms, 8cm (3¼in) below the top edge.

YOU WILL NEED
A body stocking and
a pair of socks
A large cardboard box
2 large rolls of giftwrap
Crêpe paper and clear sticky tape
All-purpose glue
80cm (31in) of hat elastic
Coloured card and scissors
A felt-tip pen

2 Cover the box with giftwrap. Join the paper in the middle of the front, top and back of the box where the joins will be covered by crêpe paper. Cut holes in the giftwrap at the head and armholes. Snip the giftwrap to the edge of the card holes. Fold the snipped edges inside the box and glue in place.

3 Cut two long strips of crêpe paper 18cm (7in) wide and glue to the front and back of the box. Make a pleat at one end of each strip, as shown, and fold neatly inside the neck hole. Glue the ends of the crêpe paper inside the box.

4 Cut a large square of coloured card for a gift tag, and cut a point at one end. Write your name on the tag with a felt-tip pen and glue it to the box.

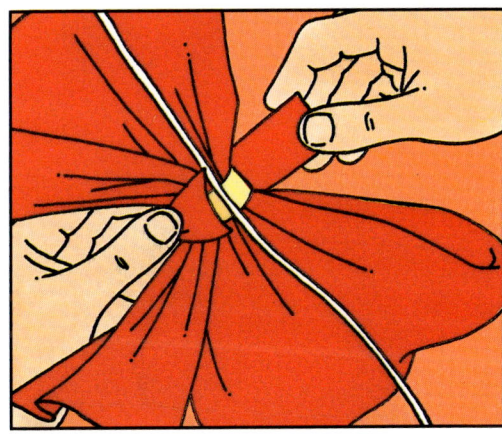

5 To make the bow head-dress, cut a strip of crêpe paper 80 x 18cm (32 x 7in). Fold the ends to the centre and glue in place. Squeeze the middle of the strip and bind with tape. For the bow tails, cut a strip of crêpe paper 50 x 18cm (20 x 7in). Tape the centre of the strip to the middle of the bow. Lay hat elastic across the back of the bow. Wrap a narrow strip of crêpe paper around the centre of the bow and secure the ends with glue.

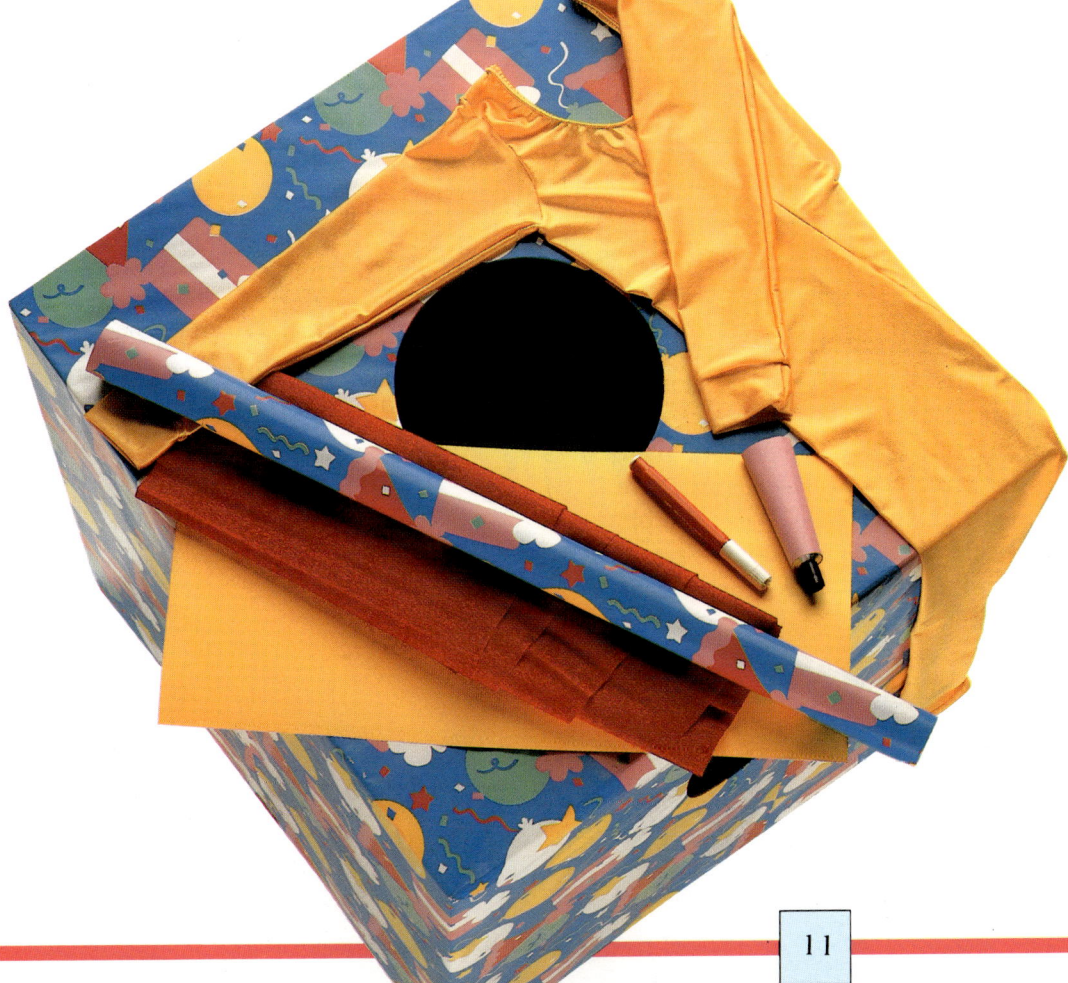

PARISIAN ARTIST

Paint the town red, or yellow or blue, in this artistic costume. Choose an old blouse or shirt for the artist's smock, and after shortening the sleeves, simply wear it back to front. The palette is made from a piece of thick card decorated with blobs of paint and the clever beard will give you that distinguished look.

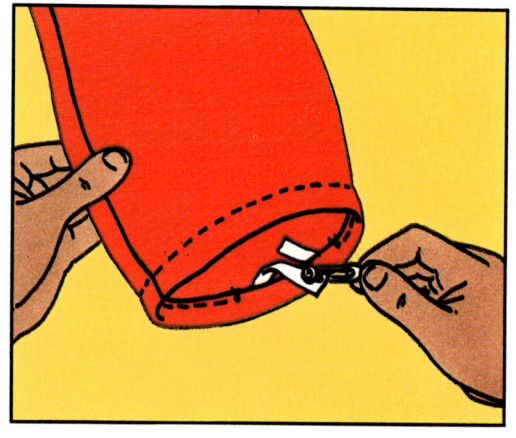

1 To make the artist's smock, cut the cuffs off the blouse sleeves. Now make a channel at the bottom of each sleeve (see page 9). Thread each channel with an 18cm (7in) length of elastic. Wear the blouse back to front with the sleeves pushed up, and a black ribbon bow sewn to the neck.

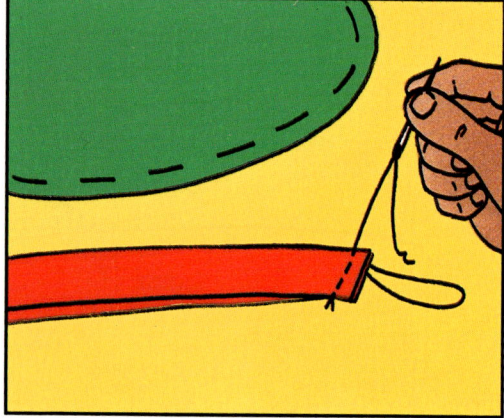

2 For the hat, cut out a 60cm (24in) circle of velvet. Sew a large running stitch around the edge of the circle. Cut a length of webbing tape long enough to fit around your head plus 3cm (1¼in). Sew the short ends together.

SAFETY TIP: *Make sure an adult helps you when using wire.*

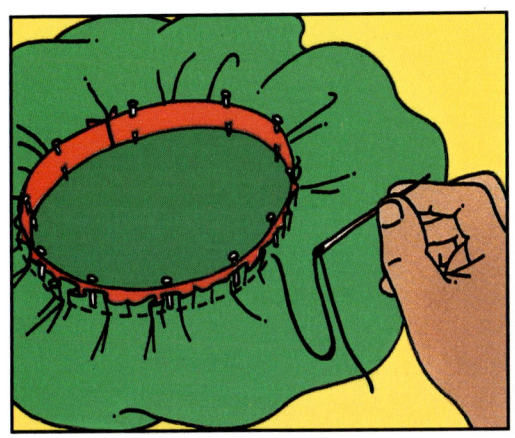

3 Gather up the circle of green velvet to fit the tape by pulling the ends of the thread. With the wrong side of the velvet on the outside, pin the tape to the inside of the gathered edge of the hat as shown. Stitch the gathers to the tape. Turn the hat right side out.

4 To make the beard, bend the wire over one ear, under your mouth and over your other ear. Ask an adult to help you do this. Remove the wire and bind the ends with masking tape so that it is comfortable to wear. Cut lots of 16cm (6½in) lengths of wool.

5 Fold the lengths of wool in half. Lay the wire over the wool and knot the wool over the wire by pulling the ends of the wool through the wool loop as shown. To finish, cut a palette from thick beige card. Squeeze blobs of acrylic paint on to the card palette and leave to harden.

YOU WILL NEED
An adult's old blouse
A pair of old trousers
70cm (28in) of green velvet
  90cm (36in) wide
36cm (14in) of elastic
60cm (24in) of webbing tape
Length of wide black ribbon
Grey wool
40cm (16in) thick wire
Masking tape
Thick beige card
Acrylic paints
Needle and thread
Scissors and tape measure
Safety pin
Sandals and paintbrush

FRIENDLY LION

You'll look like the king of the jungle in this striking outfit. The main item you need is a yellow body stocking, but you could wear a yellow T-shirt and matching tights or leggings.

1 To make the mask, trace the face and muzzle patterns on pages 78 and 79 along the solid and broken lines. Lay the tracings face down on yellow card and trace over the outlines. The patterns will appear on the card; cut out. Draw the face details with a felt-tip pen and cut out the eyes.

2 Fold the muzzle backwards along the broken lines. Rub out any pencil marks. Fold the tabs backwards and glue them under the front edges of the muzzle.

3 Fold the tabs on the face forward along the broken lines. Glue the tabs to the inside of the muzzle as shown.

4 Using a pin, make small holes at the dots on the muzzle. Poke about five whiskers into each hole. Dab glue on the ends of the whiskers to keep them in place.

6 For the tail, cut a strip of yellow fabric 70 x 11cm (28 x 4in). Fold in half and stitch the long edges together. Turn to the right side. Cut a 12cm (4½in) square of fur fabric and glue around the end of the tail. Sew the tail to the back of the body stocking.

YOU WILL NEED
A yellow body stocking
A pair of yellow socks
30cm (12in) of long-haired golden fur fabric 137cm (54in) wide
20cm (8in) of yellow fabric 90cm (36in) wide
Tracing paper and pencil
Yellow card and hat elastic
Needle, thread and scissors
Black toymaking whiskers (from craft shops)
Black felt-tip pen, glue and a pin

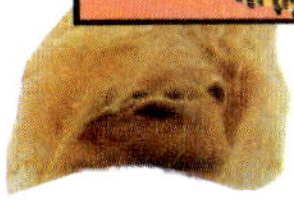

5 For the mane, cut a strip of fur fabric 137 x 12cm (54 x 4½in). Sew the short ends together on the wrong side of the fur. With a long length of double thread, sew running stitch along one long edge of the strip and gather it up into a circle (see Gathering Fabric, page 9). Glue the mane to the back of the mask. Make a hole at the dots on the mask and thread with elastic.

LITTLE DEVIL

This striking costume is perfect for a Hallowe'en party. Make the cloak from deep red satin and wear it over a dark coloured nightgown. The devil's fork is made from card, sticky-backed plastic and an old broom handle painted red.

1 To make the cloak, cut a rectangle of red satin 130cm (51in) long by 120cm (47in) wide. Hem all the edges (see page 9).

2 Turn under 1.5cm (⅝in) at each end of the bias binding and stitch in place. Pin the bias binding to the wrong side of the cloak 9cm (3½in) below one short edge. Stitch the bias binding to the cloak along the long edges to make a channel. Fix a safety pin to one end of the narrow ribbon and push it through the channel. Feel for the pin through the fabric and ease it through the channel pushing back the fabric.

YOU WILL NEED

1m 40cm (1½yd) of red satin
150cm (60in) wide
1m 80cm (2yd) of red ribbon 13mm
(½in) wide
1m 40cm (1½yd) of red ribbon 3cm
(1¼in) wide
1m 25cm (1⅜yd) of red bias binding
70cm (28in) of hat elastic
Red sticky-backed plastic
Needle and thread
Thick card and scissors
A broom handle
Tracing paper and pencil
Red poster paint and brush
Sticky tape and safety pin

3 Trace the horn pattern on page 79 and cut out the shape. Lay the pattern on to a double layer of sticky-backed plastic and keep in place with masking tape. Cut out two horns. Do not remove the backing paper on the sticky-backed plastic. Overlap the straight edges and glue together. Make a hole in both sides of each horn and thread with hat elastic. Knot the ends of the elastic over the holes.

5 Trace the tail pattern on page 79. Follow the instructions in step 3 to cut two tail ends from sticky-backed plastic. Remove the backing paper from one tail and stick the wide ribbon on to it. Stick the tails together enclosing the ribbon. Use a safety pin to attach the tail to the back of the nightgown.

4 To make the fork, cover both sides of a piece of thick card with sticky-backed plastic. Cut out a fork shape using the photograph as a guide. Paint the cut edges red. Paint the broom handle red and leave to dry. Tape the broom handle to the back of the fork.

RED INDIAN

Perfect for an outdoor party, this Red Indian outfit is made from an old shirt, fringed at the edges and worn back to front. Make false plaits from knitting wool and add lots of wooden necklaces, simple braided sandals and, of course, war-paint!

1 Using pinking shears, cut the collar, cuffs and shirt hem off the shirt. Cut a fringe along the bottom of the sleeves and along the bottom of the shirt. Using red wool, sew large cross stitches across the back of the shirt as shown. Wear the shirt back to front.

2 To make the plaits, cut lots of 55cm (22in) lengths of black wool. Divide the lengths of wool into two bunches and fasten each bunch at one end with an elastic band. Plait each bunch and secure at the bottom with an elastic band.

3 Stitch the ends of the braid together. Sew a plait to each side of the braid and turn the head-dress right side out. Cut the red fabric into seven strips 90cm (36in) long and 2cm (1in) wide. Cut one strip in half and tie each half around the bottom of the plaits. Glue three feathers to the front of the head-dress behind the braid.

4 Tie a strip of red fabric to both sides of each sandal. Now bind the sandal straps with another strip of red fabric, glueing the ends of the fabric to the straps to start and finish. When you wear the sandals bind the fabric strips around your legs and tie the ends together.

JACK-IN-THE-BOX

You can pop up at any fancy dress party with this simple Jack-in-the-box costume. If you don't have a body stocking, then a matching T-shirt and trousers or leggings will do just as well. Draw a big spring on to the body stocking with a fabric pen to make it look as if you've just sprung into action.

YOU WILL NEED
A large cardboard box
A white body stocking
Red and white card
Crêpe paper and
  sticky-backed plastic
2m (2¼yd) of green cord
3m (3¼yd) of wide
  spotted ribbon
Brass paper fasteners
Black fabric pen
Stickers
Masking tape
Soft toys
All-purpose glue
Stapler and scissors

1 To make the hat, cut a strip of red card 60 x 12.5cm (24 x 5in) and two strips of white card 60 x 2.5cm (24 x 1in). Glue the white strips along each long edge of the red strip. Overlap the ends of the strip and fasten together by pushing brass paper fasteners through the white strips, as shown. Ask an adult to help you do this. Flatten the prongs on the fasteners against the card.

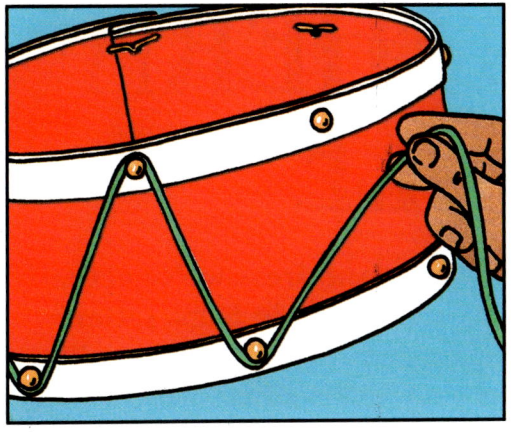

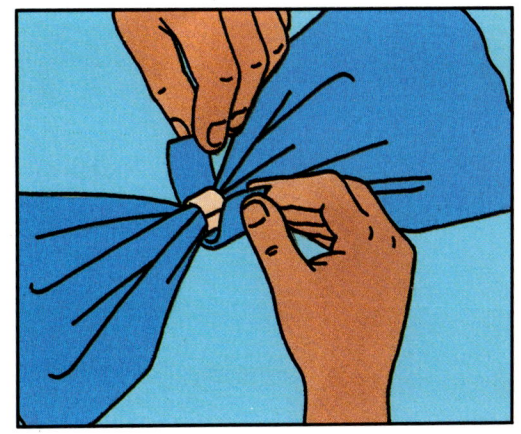

2 Push brass paper fasteners through the top white strip about 9.5cm (3¾in) apart. Push more fasteners through the lower strip between the position of the top fasteners. Bind cord up and down between the fasteners. Tie the ends of the cord together. Cover the backs of all the fasteners with masking tape.

3 To make the bow, cut a rectangle of crêpe paper 28 x 16cm (11 x 6¼in). Squeeze tight at the centre to make a bow and bind with tape. Cover the tape with a narrow strip of crêpe paper glueing the ends together at the back of the bow. Sew the bow to the neck of the body stocking.

4 Cut the flaps off the top and bottom of the box. Cover the box with sticky-backed plastic. Decorate the bow and box with stickers and shapes cut from sticky-backed plastic.

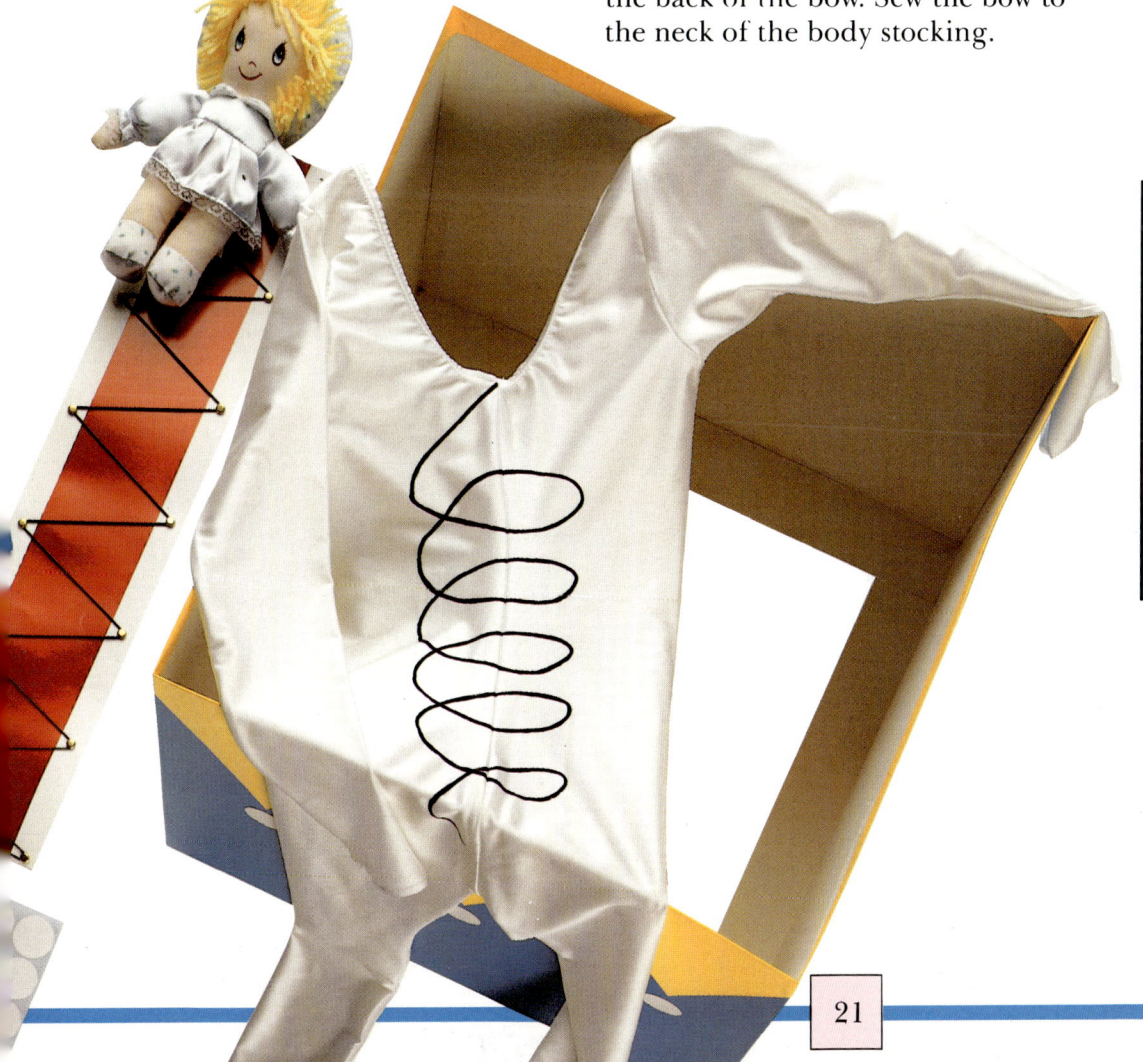

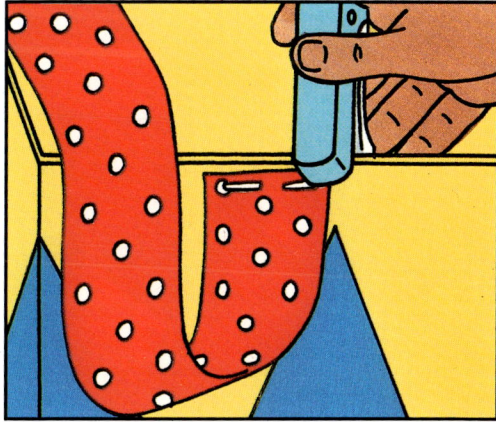

5 Cut the ribbon in half and staple one end of each piece to the top of the box at the back. Try on the box and pull the ribbons over your shoulders. Adjust the length of the ribbons and staple the other ends to the front of the box. Use masking tape to tape a few toys to the inside of the box at the top.

SOUTHERN BELLE

To make this elegant dress we've actually used shiny green dustbin bags. Often labelled as garden refuse sacks, you'll find green bags in supermarkets and garden centres. Even the rose trims are made from plastic carrier bags.

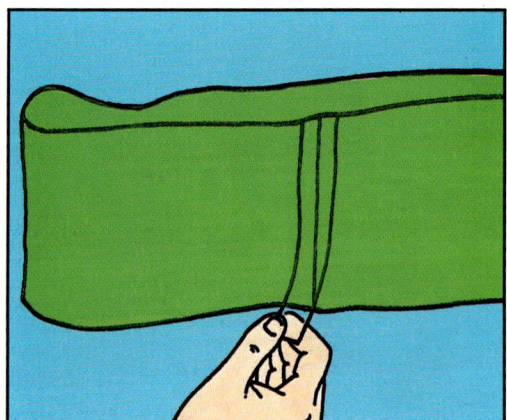

1 Cut away the neck of a T-shirt so that it is large enough to pull over your head without stretching. Next, cut two strips of plastic from a dustbin bag 90 x 18cm (36 x 7¼in). Join the short sides edge to edge with clear sticky tape.

2 To make the frill for the T-shirt, sew running stitch with a long, double length of thread along one long edge of the length of plastic, 3cm (1¼in) below the upper edge. Pull the ends of the thread to gather up the plastic and pin the frill to the neck of the T-shirt. (See Gathering Fabric, page 9.) Pull up the gathers to fit and stitch the frill to the T-shirt.

3 To make the skirt, cut two rectangles of plastic from dustbin bags 80 x 50cm (31 x 20in). Join the short sides edge to edge with clear sticky tape to make one long strip. (Continued on the next page.)

YOU WILL NEED
A T-shirt and a pair of gloves
Coloured dustbin bags and plastic carrier bags.
Red sticky-backed plastic
80cm (31in) of ribbon
Double-sided sticky tape and clear sticky tape
Needle and thread
Stapler
Scissors and tape measure
Child's umbrella
Stick-on Velcro
2 hair combs

4 For the waistband, cut a strip of sticky-backed plastic 5cm (2in) wide and long enough to fit around your waist plus 5cm (2in). Stick a strip of double-sided tape along one long edge of the backing paper. Gradually peel the backing paper off the double-sided tape and stick one long edge of the skirt on to the waistband, gathering up the plastic to fit.

5 To make the skirt frill, cut three rectangles of plastic from dustbin bags 80 x 44cm (31 x 17in). Join the short sides edge to edge with clear sticky tape to make one long strip. Sew running stitch along one long edge of the strip, 3cm (1¼in) below the upper edge and gather up the plastic, as in step 2.

6 Pin the frill on to the lower edge of the skirt. Gently pull up the gathers to fit and sew in place. Stick the skirt and the frill together at the back with clear sticky tape. Fasten the ends of the waistband together with stick-on Velcro.

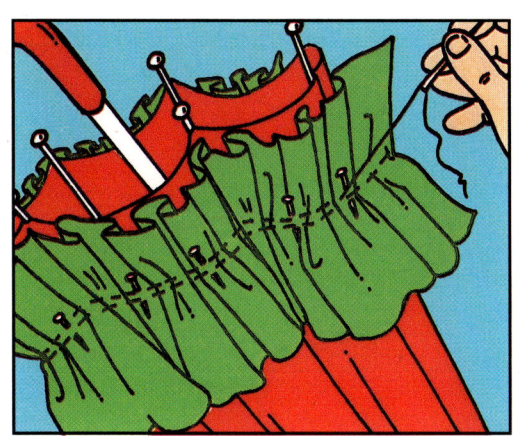

7 To make the frill for the parasol, cut three strips of plastic from dustbin bags 1m x 12cm (40 x 5in). Join the short sides together with clear sticky tape to make one long strip. Sew running stitch along the centre of the strip and gather up the plastic as before. Pin the frill to the umbrella and gently pull up the gathers to fit. Sew in place. Tie ribbon in a bow around the handle.

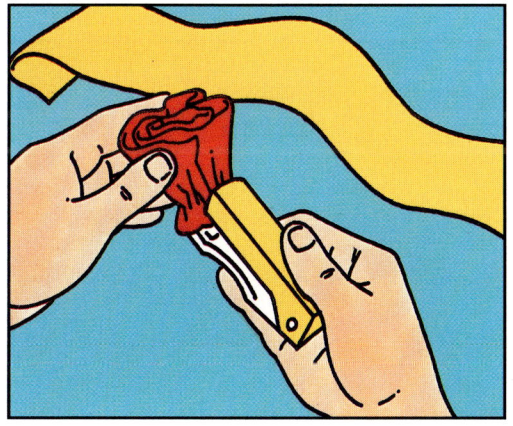

8 For the roses, cut strips from coloured plastic carrier bags 50 x 13cm (19 x 5in) for large roses and 35 x 8cm (14 x 3¼in) for small roses. Fold the strips lengthwise in half. Starting at one end, coil the strips making little pleats on the lower long edges and staple the lower edges together at intervals. Sew a few small roses to the gloves, the parasol and hair combs. Sew large and small roses to the T-shirt and skirt.

STRONGMAN

If you wear this super strongman outfit to a fancy dress party we can guarantee you'll be the main attraction. Use face paints to add a bushy moustache and some colourful tattoos, and you're ready to go!

1 To make the tunic, you will first need to make a full-size paper pattern following the diagram on page 80. To find out how to do this and how to cut out fabric read the instructions on page 8. Now cut out two fur fabric tunic shapes, and cut a ragged edge along the bottom of both.

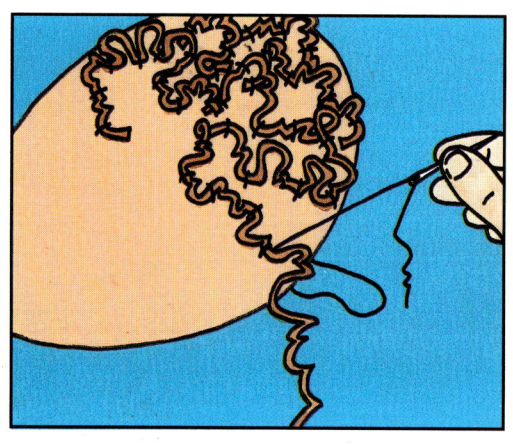

3 For the hairy chest, cut out a large oval of stockinette. Arrange strands of wool on top and stitch in place. Stick the hairy chest to your chest with double-sided tape.

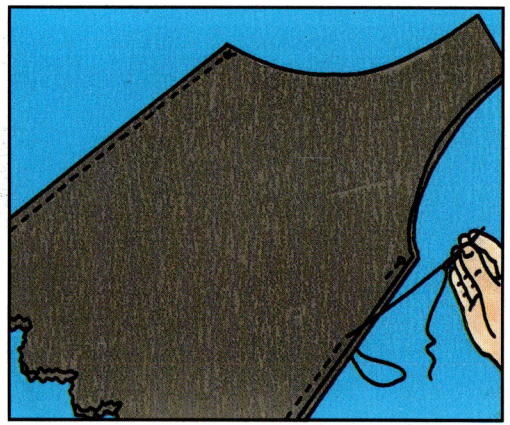

2 Pin the tunic shapes together, right sides facing, and stitch them together along the side seams and across the shoulder using running stitch (see page 8).

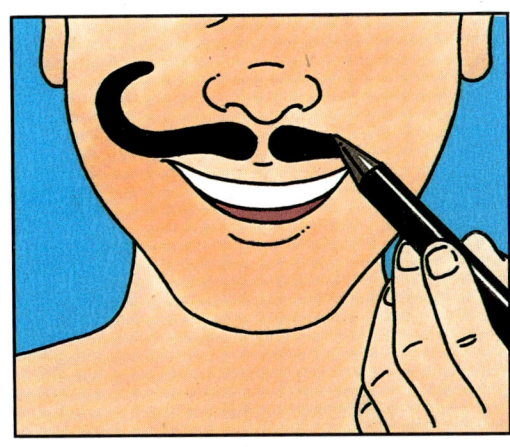

4 To make the dumb-bells, ask an adult to cut a 45cm (18in) length of broom handle. Stick a rubber ball to each end of the broom handle. Paint the balls and the broom handle black. Leave to dry.

5 To complete your outfit, use face paints to give yourself a bushy moustache and to draw some colourful tattoos on your arms.

YOU WILL NEED
1m (40in) of fur fabric
  137cm (54in) wide
Stockinette and brown wool
Double-sided tape
2 rubber balls
Length of broom handle
All-purpose glue
Black paint and paintbrush
Needle and thread
Scissors

MR SCARECROW

This colourful outfit is really easy to put together and it looks great. You will need some old clothes and a pair of Wellington boots. If you don't have these at home you can buy them cheaply from a local second-hand clothes shop.

2 To make the neck scarf, cut out a square of fabric. Fray the edges by pulling out three or four strands of fabric.

1 Cut a ragged edge around the sleeves of the old shirt and around the legs of the old pair of trousers. Cut out patches of colourful fabric and sew them to the shirt and trousers. Glue pieces of straw to the bottom of the shirt sleeves.

YOU WILL NEED
An old shirt, a pair of trousers and a hat
Scraps of fabric and straw
A pair of Wellington boots
Orange card and scissors
Tracing paper and pencil
Hat elastic and 2cm (1in) wide elastic
All-purpose glue, needle and thread

3 Cut two lengths of wide elastic long enough to wrap around the tops of the Wellington boots. Sew pieces of straw to the elastic. Overlap the ends of the elastic and sew them together. Slip over the tops of the Wellington boots.

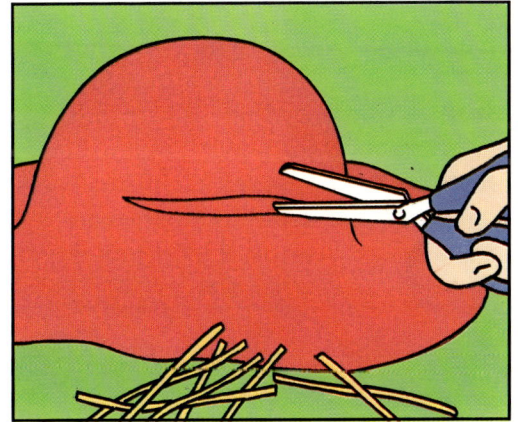

4 Cut a slit across the crown or top section of the hat. Glue straw inside the hat and pull it through the slit. Glue more straw inside the brim of the hat so that it hangs down.

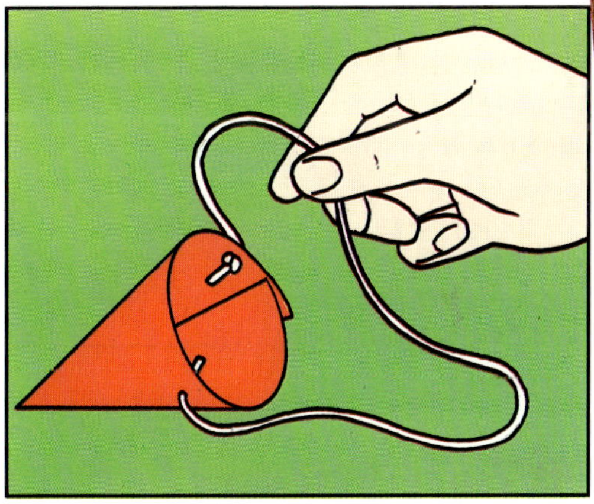

5 To make the nose, trace the pattern on page 80. Turn your tracing over and lay it on to the orange card. Rub firmly over the outline with a pencil. The pattern will appear on the card. Cut out the nose, overlap the straight edges and glue together. Make a hole at each side of the nose. Thread elastic through the holes and knot the ends over the holes.

RAG DOLL

Look for some bright spotty fabric to make this colourful rag doll dress. If you have a sewing machine at home, ask an adult to help you use it to sew up the side seams instead of sewing them by hand. An old pair of tights and some wool are used to make the chunky plaits, trimmed with large floppy bows. Use face paints to give yourself rosy cheeks and long eyelashes.

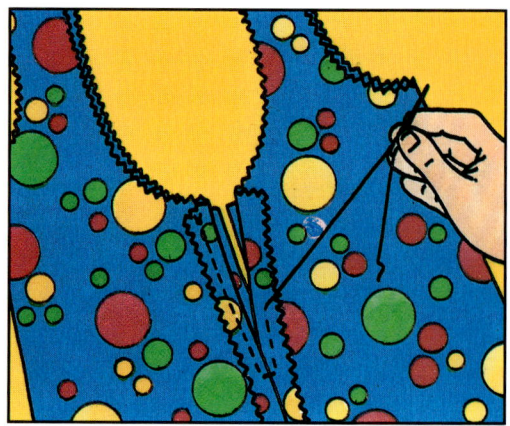

2 Fold over the raw edges at the top of the side seams and sew in place as shown. Cut the narrow ribbon into quarters and sew one piece to the top of each underarm edge. Turn the dress right side out and sew lace around the bottom edge.

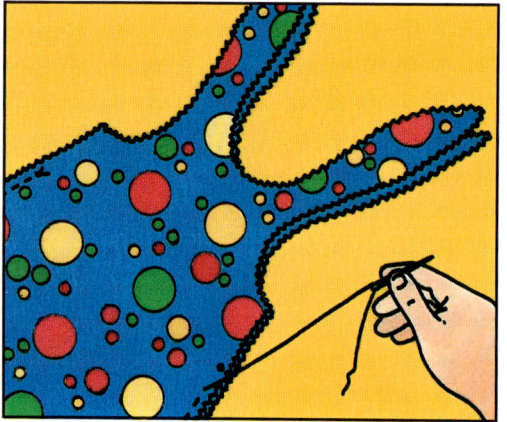

1 To make the dress, you will first need to make a full-size paper pattern following the diagram on page 81. To find out how to do this and how to cut out fabric read the instructions on page 8. Now cut out two dress pieces from spotted fabric using pinking shears. Pin the pieces together, right sides facing, and sew along the side seams using running stitch (see page 8). Leave a 10cm (4in) gap below each armhole.

SAFETY TIP: *Make sure an adult helps you when using wire.*

3 For the wig, cut the legs off a pair of tights. Match the front and back seams and stitch across the cut edge in a curve to make a skull cap. Turn the cap right side out.

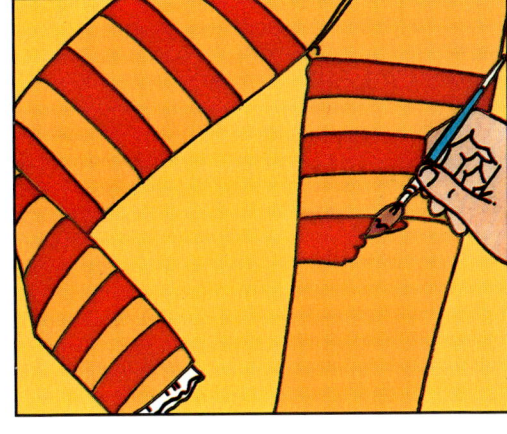

4 Cut lots of 100cm (40in) lengths of wool. Sew the middle of each length of wool to the seam of the skull cap. Try on the wig and gather the 'hair' into a bunch at each side of your face. Tie a length of wool around the top of each bunch. Take the wig off and plait the bunches. Fasten the ends together with an elastic band.

6 To paint stripes on the leggings, push a plastic bag down into the legs so that the fabric paint does not seep through to the other side. Paint stripes on one side of the leggings with fabric paint. Leave to dry then paint the other side. Cut the wide blue ribbon in half and tie into bows. Glue the bows to your shoes.

5 Bind the ends of the wire with masking tape. Bend one end of each piece of wire into a loop and, starting at the top of the plait, push the other end of the wire down through the plait. Sew the looped end of the wire to the skull cap. Cut the wide green ribbon in half and tie a bow around the bottom of each plait to hide the elastic band.

TV SET

This is the perfect costume for all budding television personalities. A large cardboard box is all that is needed for the case. Keep the background plain and wear a colourful T-shirt to make the picture really stand out. Make a wire TV aerial and top the box with a plant or a bowl of artificial fruit.

1 Cut the flaps from the bottom of the box. Now cut a square out of one side of the box for the television screen. Paint the box grey and leave to dry. Glue a square of blue card to the inside back of the box for the background.

2 Glue the buttons in a row down one side of the box for the TV controls. To make an aerial, bend the wire into a circular shape with the ends pointing down. Ask an adult to help you do this.

SAFETY TIP: *Make sure an adult helps you when using wire.*

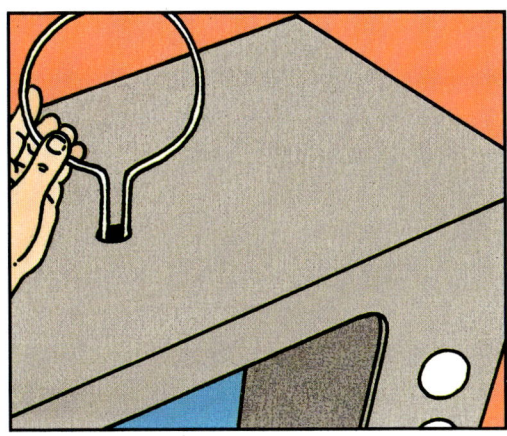

3 Pierce a hole in the top of the box with a knitting needle. You may need some help with this. Push the ends of the aerial into the hole. Bend the ends of the wire flat against the top of the box on the inside. Tape the wire in place.

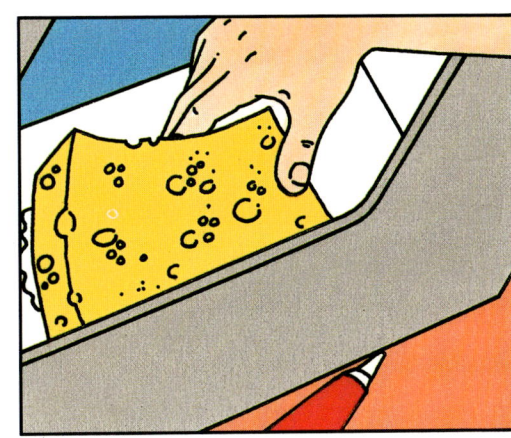

4 To make the TV set comfortable to wear, glue a square of foam to the inside top of the box. Position the foam in the centre so it will rest on your head. To finish, glue an artificial plant pot to the top of the television.

YOU WILL NEED

T-shirt and trousers
A large cardboard box
Blue card
Thick wire
15cm (6in) square of thick foam or a bath sponge
4 flat buttons
Grey poster paint and paintbrush
Knitting needle
All-purpose glue
Scissors and sticky tape
Artificial pot plant

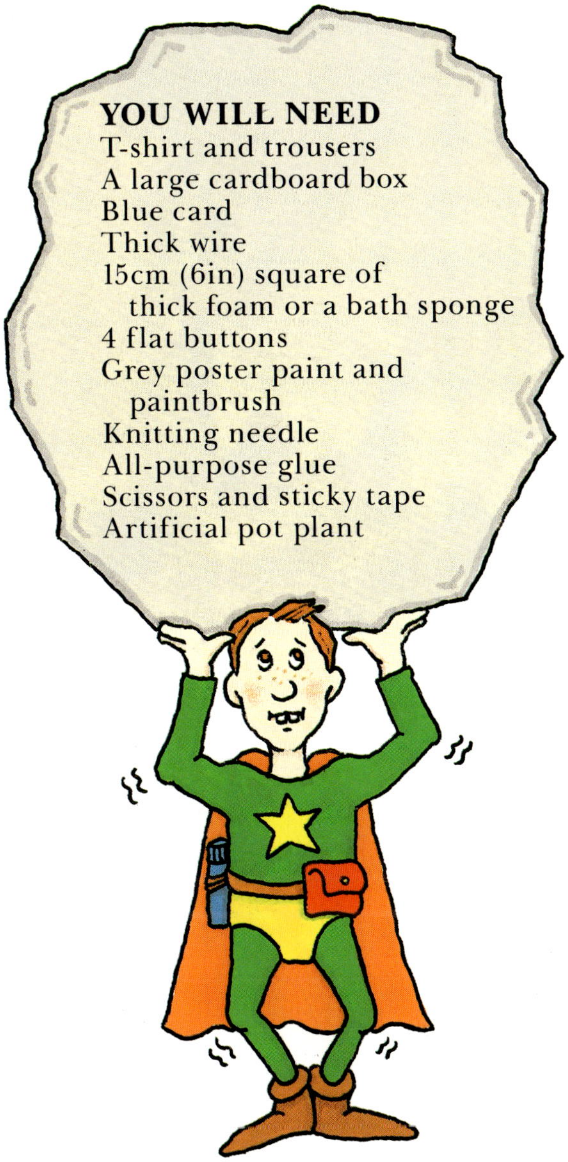

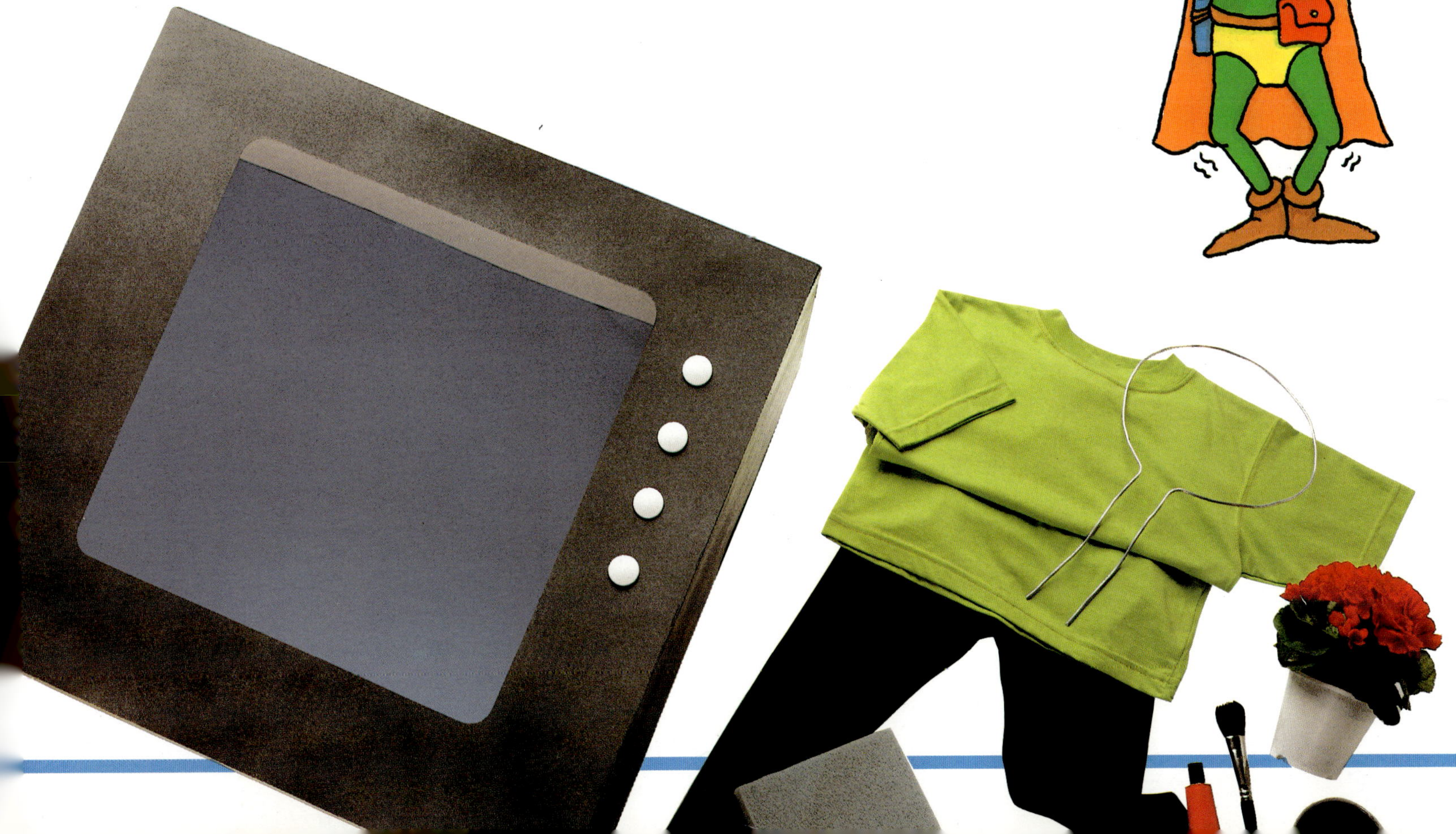

FLOWER FAIRIES

Flower fairies come in every colour available. Use pink or mauve fabric to make the dress as shown here, or choose a colour that matches a leotard you already have. You may want to ask an adult to help you make this costume as it is a little more difficult than most of the others featured in the book. If you have a sewing machine at home ask an adult to help you use it to sew up the fabric.

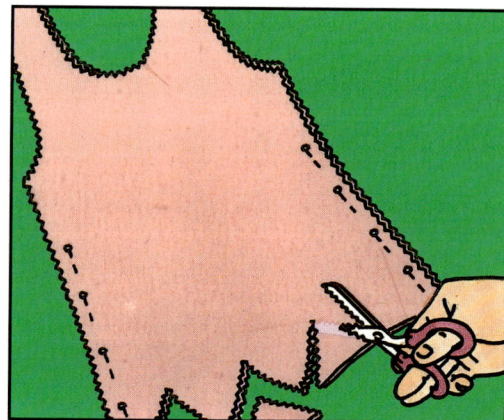

1 To make the dress, you will first need to make a full-size paper pattern following the diagram on page 81. To find out how to do this and how to cut out fabric read the instructions on page 8. Now cut out four dress pieces from organza using pinking shears. Pin the dress pieces together in pairs and cut a scalloped edge to look like petals along the bottom of each pair.

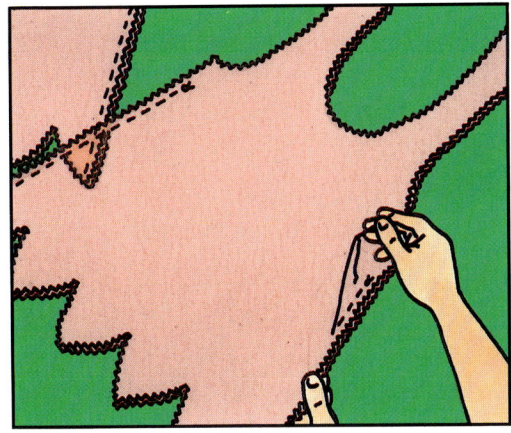

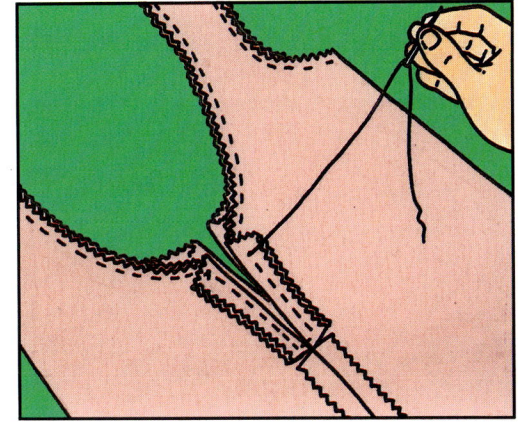

2 Now sew each pair of dresses together along the side seams using running stitch (see page 8). Leave a 10cm (4in) gap below each armhole as shown. Snip the fabric to the seam at the start of the gap.

3 Slip one dress inside the other matching the armholes and the gap at the top of the side seams. Stitch the armholes, neck edges and shoulder straps together close to the raw edges, or fold the fabric over and stitch in place. Fold over the double layer of fabric at the top of the side seams and sew in place as shown.

YOU WILL NEED

A leotard
4m 30cm (4¾yd) of organza 90cm (36in) wide
1m 20cm (48in) of ribbon
Silk flowers and leaves
Pink and green crêpe paper
Thick and fine wire
Florists' tape
Clear sticky tape
All-purpose glue
Scissors and pinking shears
Needle and thread

(Continued on the next page.)

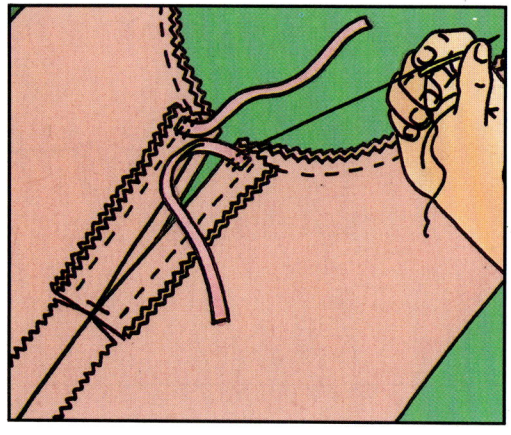

4 Cut the ribbon into four equal lengths and sew one piece to the top of each underarm edge, as shown. Turn the dress right side out. When you wear the dress tie the pieces of ribbon together in a bow under each arm and tie the shoulder straps together.

6 To make the head-dress, ask an adult to cut a length of thick wire large enough to wrap around your head. Overlap the ends of the wire and bind together with florists' tape. Attach small silk flowers to the head-dress with florists' tape. Make bracelets and ankle bracelets in the same way.

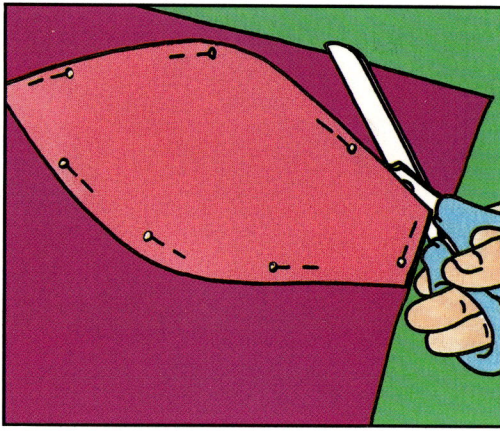

7 For the hat, make a full-size paper pattern following the petal diagram on page 80. Pin the pattern on to pink crêpe paper and cut out one petal. Repeat to cut out a further nine petals.

5 Cut the heads off the large silk flowers and sew them around the neck of the of the dress at the front. Sew some smaller flowers between the large flowers.

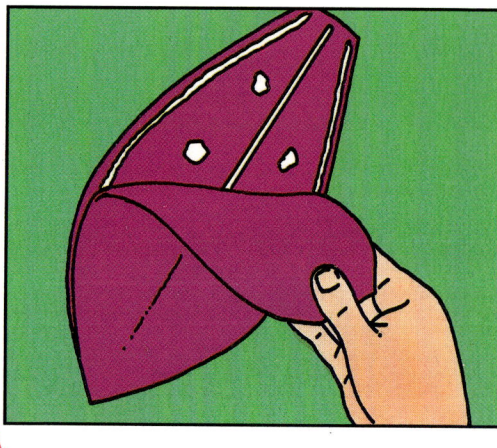

8 Now cut five lengths of fine wire 25cm (10in) long. Spread glue on five of the petals and lay a length of wire down the centre of each one. Press one of the remaining petals to each glued petal, enclosing the wire.

SAFETY TIP: *Make sure an adult helps you when using wire.*

9 Join the petals together edge-to-edge at the top and stick strips of tape across the joins as shown. Bend the points of the petals upwards.

10 Squeeze the top of the petals tightly together to make a hat shape and bind with sticky tape. Glue silk leaves around the top of the hat. Glue a narrow strip of green crêpe paper around the bound top.

PIRATE

All you need is a waistcoat to turn a striped T-shirt and spotted scarf into an authentic pirate outfit. Add a black eye patch, a moustache and an earring to complete the costume. You'll also need to arm yourself with a sabre and telescope in case of enemy ships. Look out for these in toy shops.

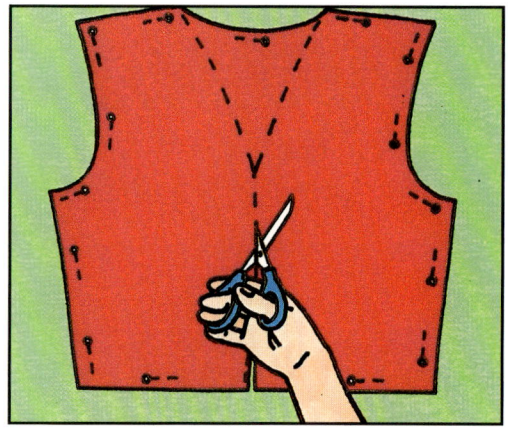

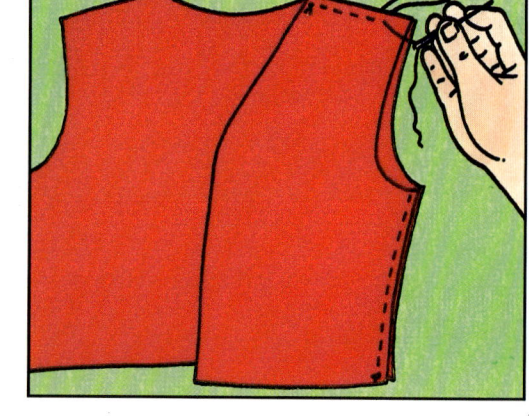

2 Stitch the front pieces to the back along the side seams and shoulder seams, as shown. Turn the waistcoat right side out and sew the buttons to the front edges.

1 To make the waistcoat, you will first need to make a full size paper pattern following the diagram on page 82. To find out how to do this and how to cut out fabric read the instructions on page 8. Now cut out two waistcoat shapes from felt along the solid lines shown on the pattern. Pin the paper pattern back on to one of the shapes and cut the felt along the broken lines to give two front pieces.

YOU WILL NEED
A striped T-shirt
A pair of old trousers
A spotted headscarf
40cm (16in) of felt
90cm (36in) wide
6 gold buttons and a black belt
70cm (28in) of hat elastic
Black card
A brass curtain ring
Clip-on earring back
Double-sided sticky tape
Needle and thread
Scissors

3 Cut an eye patch from black card. Make a hole at each side and thread with elastic. Knot the ends of the elastic together.

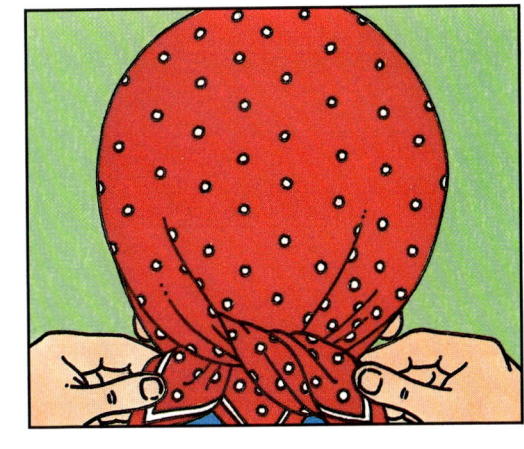

5 Fold the scarf diagonally in half, place it across your forehead and knot the ends together at the back, as shown. To make an earring, attach a brass curtain ring to a clip-on earring back. To finish your costume, cut a ragged edge along the bottom of the trouser legs and wear them with a black belt.

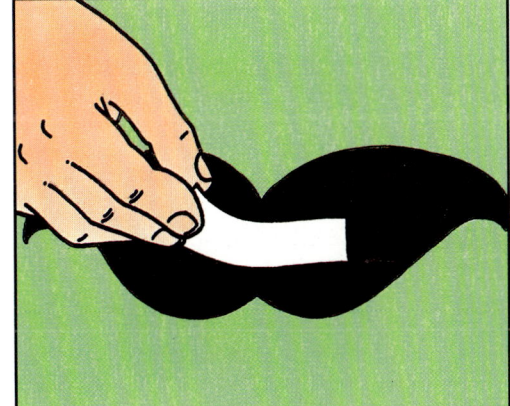

4 Cut a moustache from black card. Stick a length of double-sided tape on the back and stick the moustache just above your upper lip.

ICE MAIDEN

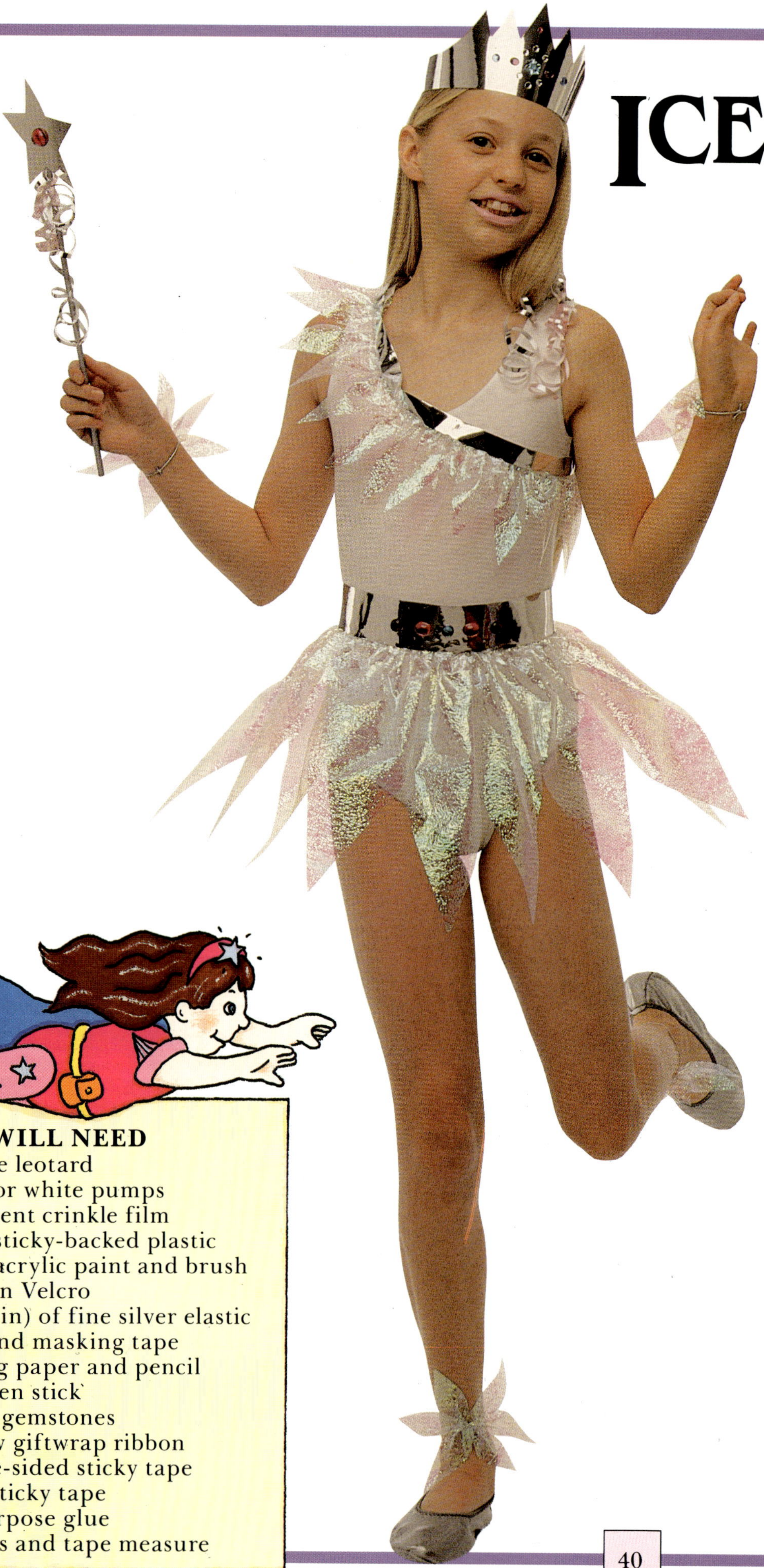

Stay cool in this beautiful icy costume which sparkles with every move. A white leotard or swimming costume is the base for the outfit decorated with an eye-catching iridescent skirt and shoulder frill. Add a pair of silver pumps, a wand and a crown to complete the sophisticated look.

YOU WILL NEED
A white leotard
Silver or white pumps
Iridescent crinkle film
Silver sticky-backed plastic
Silver acrylic paint and brush
Stick-on Velcro
1m (40in) of fine silver elastic
Card and masking tape
Tracing paper and pencil
A garden stick
Plastic gemstones
Narrow giftwrap ribbon
Double-sided sticky tape
Clear sticky tape
All-purpose glue
Scissors and tape measure

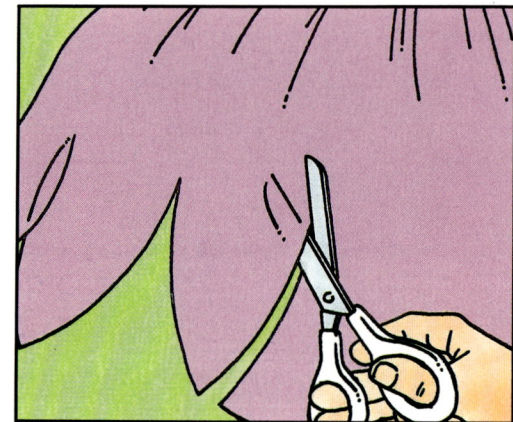

1 Cut a strip of iridescent film 180cm (70in) long by 30cm (12in) wide for the skirt and a second strip 180cm (70in) long by 12cm (5in) wide for the shoulder frill. Join the pieces of film with tape if necessary. Cut points along one long edge of the skirt and the frill.

4 To make the crown, cover both sides of a piece of card with silver sticky-backed plastic. Trace the pattern on page 82 and extend the sides so that the crown will fit your head. Cut out the pattern and tape it to the silver covered card. Cut out the crown and glue the ends together. For the wand, cut out a star from the silver card. Paint the garden stick silver and glue giftwrap ribbon to the top. Glue the star to the stick. Glue gemstones to the crown, star and waistband.

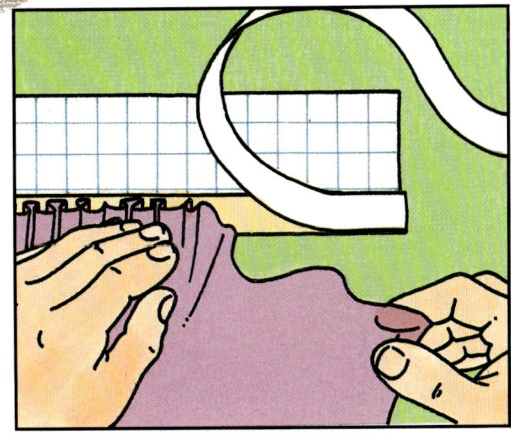

2 For the waistband, cut a strip of silver sticky-backed plastic 5cm (2in) wide and long enough to fit around your waist plus 5cm (2in). Cut another strip 78cm (31in) long by 2cm (¾in) wide for the shoulder band. Stick double-sided tape along one long edge of the backing paper on the waistband and the shoulder band. Do not remove the backing paper on the sticky-backed plastic.

3 To make the skirt, gradually peel the backing paper off the double-sided tape on the waistband and stick the long, straight edge of the skirt to the tape. Gather up the skirt to fit. Join the frill to the shoulder band in the same way. Fasten the ends of the waistband and the shoulder band with Velcro.

5 For the ankle and wrist decorations, cut four 18cm (7in) squares of iridescent film. Cut points along two opposite edges of each square. Cut the elastic into quarters and tie each piece tightly around the centre of a square. Knot the elastic around your wrists and ankles. To finish, stick giftwrap ribbon to one shoulder of the leotard.

SPACE HEROES

A body-hugging leotard and a pair of leggings are the main ingredients for this space-age outfit. A pair of rubber boots painted silver and decorated with shiny stars will complete the look. The collar, waistband and gauntlets are all made from silver sticky-backed plastic that has the backing paper left on.

1 To make the collar, cut a rectangle of silver sticky-backed plastic 46 x 41cm (18 x 16in). The long edges are the front and back of the collar. Cut a square in the middle of the collar big enough to fit around your neck. Now cut from the centre back of the collar to the edge of the neck square. To fasten the collar, stick Velcro to the edges.

2 Cut a decorative edge along the sides of the collar as shown, but leave a long tab of sticky-backed plastic at the top and bottom of each side. When you wear the collar stick the tabs together under your arms with Velcro. Do not remove the backing paper on the sticky-backed plastic. Cut a star from coloured sticky-backed plastic and stick to the front of the collar.

3 To make the gauntlets, trace the pattern on page 83 and cut out. Lay the pattern on to a double layer of silver sticky-backed plastic and keep in place with sticky tape. Cut out two gauntlets. Decorate each gauntlet with a star cut from coloured sticky-backed plastic. Fasten the edges of the gauntlets around your wrists with stick-on Velcro.

4 For the belt, cut a strip of silver sticky-backed plastic 5cm (2in) wide and long enough to fit around your waist plus 5cm (2in). Do not remove the backing paper on the sticky-backed plastic. Fasten the ends of the belt together with Velcro. Paint the boots silver. Decorate each boot with a star cut from coloured sticky-backed plastic.

5 To make the head-dress, stick silver sticky-backed plastic to card and cut out a star shape. Stick the star to the centre of the narrow ribbon with double-sided tape. Tie the ribbon around your head with the star at the front.

YOU WILL NEED
A leotard and leggings
A pair of Wellington boots
Silver sticky-backed plastic
Pink or blue sticky-backed plastic
1m 30cm (1½yd) of
    narrow ribbon
Double-sided tape
Stick-on Velcro
Silver poster paint and
    paintbrush
Thin card and sticky tape
Tracing paper and pencil
Scissors

BLACK CAT

A black body stocking or a T-shirt and tights are the main essentials for this feline outfit. Add a fluffy white tummy and soft ears to make the costume look more realistic. The nose is made from a single section of an egg carton, tied on with elastic. A toy mouse to play with completes the look.

2 For the nose, cut a section from the egg carton. Paint the section white and leave it to dry. Draw on a muzzle with a red felt-tip pen. Make three small holes at each side of the nose and push about five whiskers into each hole. Dab glue on the ends of the whiskers to keep them in place. Make another hole at each side of the nose close to the edge and thread with hat elastic.

1 To make the head-dress, trace the ear pattern on page 83, and cut out. Pin the pattern on to a double layer of pink felt and cut out two ear shapes. Remove the pattern and pin it to the back of the black fur fabric. Cut out one ear and then repeat to cut out a second ear. Stitch a felt ear to the wrong side of a fur ear. Do not stitch across the bottom edge. Turn the ears to the right side and pin to the hairband. Sew in place.

SAFETY TIP: *Make sure an adult helps you when using wire.*

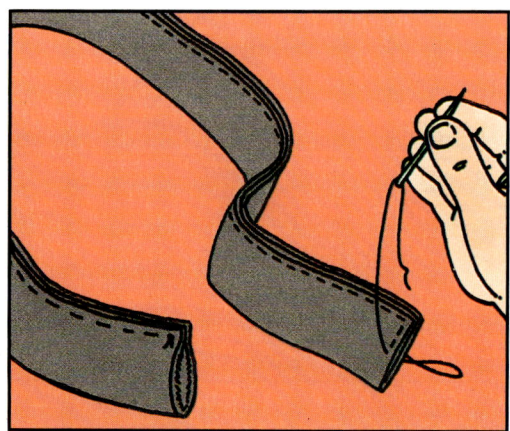

3 Cut out a large oval of white fur fabric for the tummy and sew to the body stocking. For the tail, cut a strip of black fur fabric 70cm (28in) long by 12cm (5in) wide. Fold in half lengthwise, wrong sides together. Stitch along the long edge and across one end. Turn the tail right side out.

4 Bind the ends of the wire with masking tape and then bend the ends into a loop. Ask an adult to help you do this. Slip the tail over the wire and sew the end of the wire and the open end of the tail to the back of the body stocking. To finish, cut out pink felt paw pads and glue to the palms of the gloves.

YOU WILL NEED
A black body stocking
A pair of black gloves
A black velvet hairband
40cm (16in) of white fur fabric
70cm (28in) of black fur fabric
Pink felt and hat elastic
Cardboard egg carton
70cm (28in) thick wire
White poster paint and paintbrush
A red felt-tip pen
Black toymaking whiskers
   (from craft shops)
All-purpose glue
Masking tape, scissors and pins
Needle and thread
Tracing paper and pencil

GRANDFATHER CLOCK

You'll be sure to get to the party on time in this unusual Grandfather Clock costume. The brown moiré fabric has a wood-effect pattern which is perfect for the clock case. If you have a sewing machine at home, ask an adult to help you use it to sew the side seams together instead of sewing them by hand. To complete the costume, glue toy mice to the tunic and the head-dress.

1 Using a pencil, trace the clock pattern on page 84 and cut out the circle. Do not cut out the hands. Pin the pattern on to the square of white fabric and cut out the shape. Copy the Roman numerals shown on the pattern on to the clock face using a fabric pen. Leave to dry.

2 To make the tunic, you will first need to make a full-size paper pattern following the diagram on page 86. To find out how to do this and how to cut out fabric read the instructions on page 8. Now cut out two tunics from moiré fabric using pinking shears.

3 Glue the clock face to the front of one of the tunics, 5cm (2in) below the neck edge. Glue or sew gold cord around the edge of the clock face.

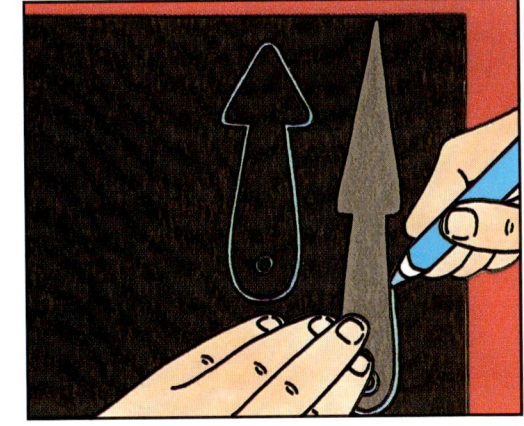

4 Now cut out the tracings of the clock hands. Position them on the black card and draw around the shapes with a coloured pencil. Cut out the hands. Make a hole at the dots on the hands and through the centre of the clock face with scissor points. Ask an adult to help you.

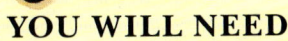

YOU WILL NEED
3m (3½yd) of brown moiré
    fabric 90cm (36in) wide
30cm (12in) of white fabric
90cm (1yd) of gold cord
60cm (24in) of brown ribbon
Brown, black and gold card
A black fabric pen
A brass paper fastener
Tracing paper and pencil
A sticking-plaster
Pinking shears and scissors
All-purpose glue
Needle and thread

(Continued on the next page.)

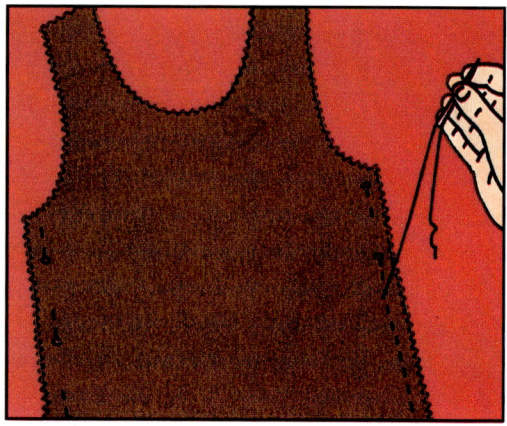

6 Pin the two tunics together right sides facing. Stitch them together along the side seams using running stitch (see page 8).

5 Push a brass paper fastener through the holes on the hands and then through the clock face. Open out the prongs on the underside of the clock and flatten against the fabric. Stick a plaster over the prongs so that the tunic is comfortable to wear.

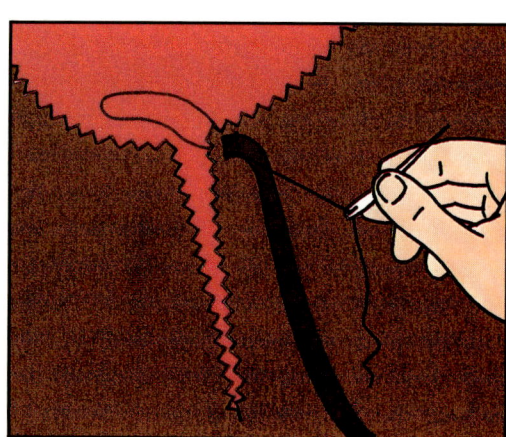

7 Cut a slit about 10cm (4in) long from the neck edge of the back tunic with pinking shears. Cut the ribbon in half and sew a length to each side of the slit. Tie the ribbon in a bow when you wear the costume. Turn the tunic right side out.

9. Now lay the pattern of the small moulding on to gold card and draw around it. Cut out the shape and lay it back on the card. Draw around the shape and cut out a second moulding. Glue one of the mouldings to the brown moiré clock top. Cut a strip of brown card 60cm (24in) long and 2cm (1in) wide. Glue the ends together and glue the clock top to the front of the strip.

8. To make the head-dress, trace the patterns for the clock top and the small moulding on page 85 and cut out. Lay the pattern of the clock top on to brown card and draw around the shape with a pencil. Cut out the shape. Gluc the brown card clock top on to moiré fabric and trim away the fabric from around the edges.

10. Glue the second small gold moulding to the tunic just below the clock. Trace the pattern of the large moulding on page 85 and cut out. Lay the pattern on to gold card and draw around it. Cut out the shape and glue it to the bottom of the tunic. To finish, glue toy mice to the tunic and the head-dress.

WICKED WITCH

From the ugly green nose to the long witchy fingernails this is the perfect outfit for Hallowe'en! Make or borrow a twig broom and decorate your costume with plastic creepy crawlies bought from a joke shop to add the finishing touches. Choose face paints in green and black to make sure you look suitably bewitching on the night.

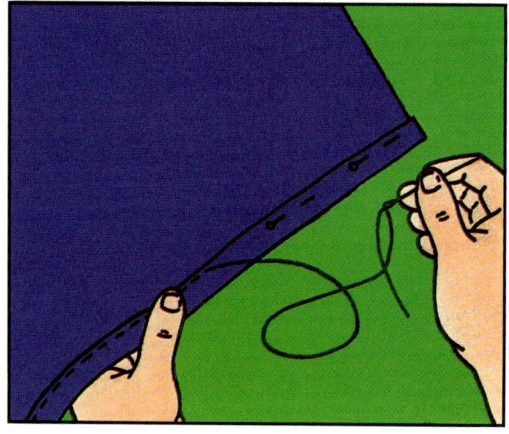

1 To make the cloak, cut a piece of purple fabric 120cm (47in) square. Make a hem on two opposite edges (see page 9).

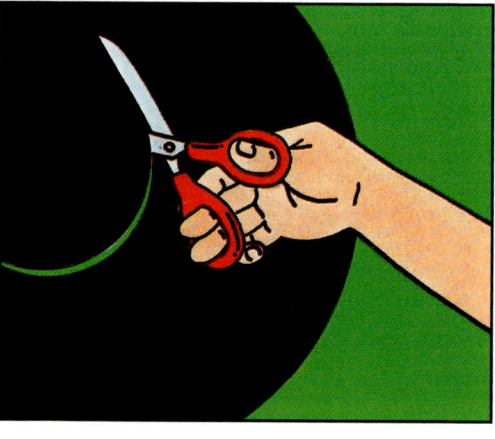

3 To make the hat, cut out a 38cm (15in) diameter circle of black felt for the brim. Cut a 14cm (5½in) diameter hole in the centre of the circle.

4 For the cone, draw a full-size paper pattern following the diagram on page 86. Cut out the pattern and pin it to black felt. Cut out the cone shape. Spray the cone and the brim with starch and ask an adult to help you press them.

2 Now make a channel on one raw edge of the cloak (see page 9). Thread the channel with cord. This is the top edge of the cloak. Cut a jagged edge along the bottom edge of the cloak and nightgown.

SAFETY TIP: *Make sure an adult helps you when using an iron.*

5 Fold the cone in half and sew the straight edges together. Pin the cone into the hole in the brim and stitch in place as shown. Cut lots of lengths of green wool and glue inside the hat for hair. Stuff tissue paper into the top of the cone to make it stand upright.

6 For the nose, trace the pattern on page 86. Lay the tracing face down on green card and rub over the outline with a pencil. The pattern will appear on the card; cut out. Fold the nose backwards along the fold line shown on the pattern. Glue the tab under the opposite side. Make a hole at either side of the nose and thread with elastic. Cut long nails from green card and stick to your nails with double-sided tape.

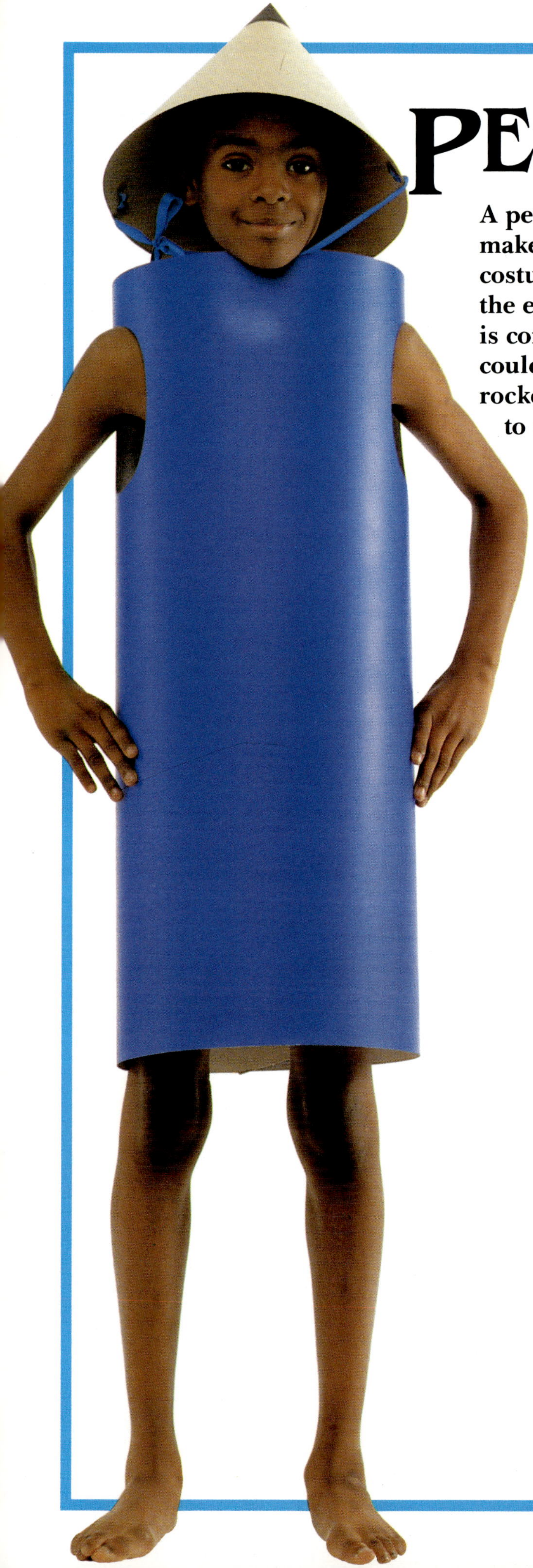

PENCIL PERSON

A pencil body with a pencil point hat makes a very simple yet effective costume. Ask a friend to help you overlap the edges of the costume to make sure it is comfortable and not crooked. You could also turn this shape into a firework rocket with a trail of glittery decorations to add sparkle.

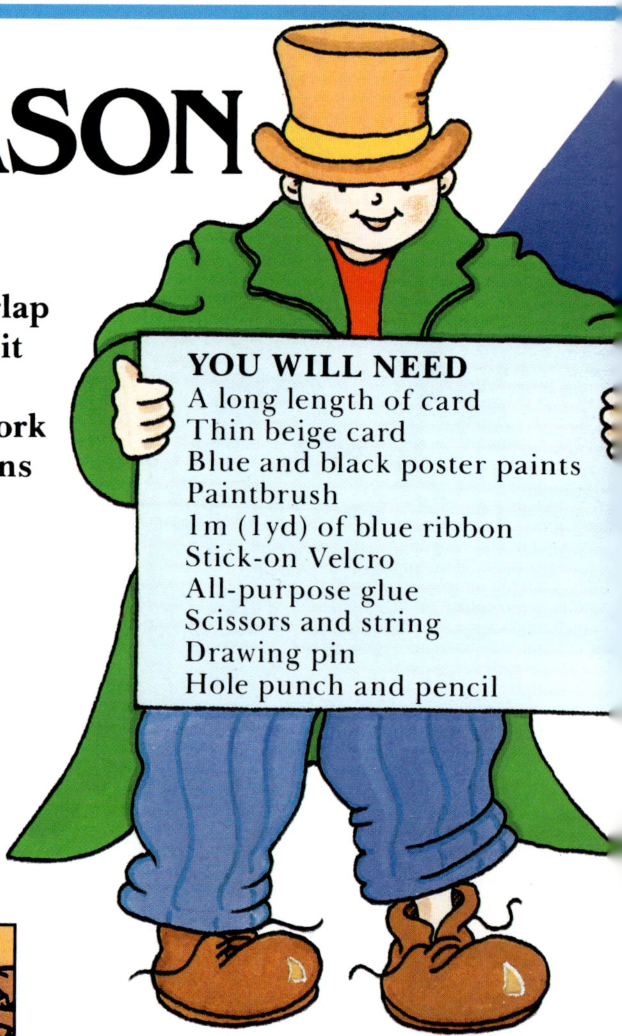

YOU WILL NEED
A long length of card
Thin beige card
Blue and black poster paints
Paintbrush
1m (1yd) of blue ribbon
Stick-on Velcro
All-purpose glue
Scissors and string
Drawing pin
Hole punch and pencil

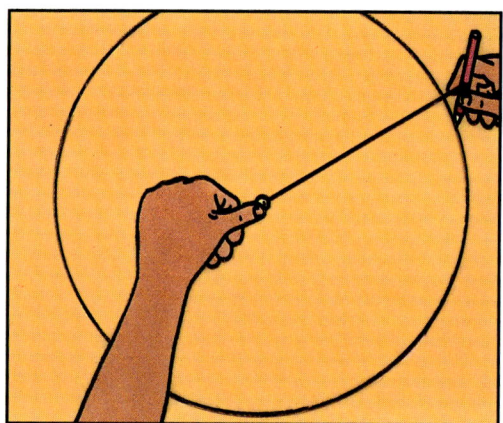

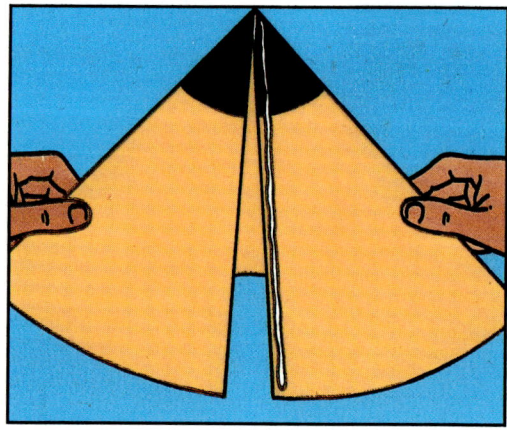

1 To make the pencil point hat, tie a length of string to a drawing pin. Now tie a pencil to the string 28cm (11in) away from the drawing pin. Position the beige card on a work surface. Press the drawing pin into the centre of the card and carefully draw a circle as shown.

2 Draw a line across the centre of the circle and cut out one half circle. Draw a semicircle at the centre of the straight edge. Lay the hat shape on to a flat surface and paint the area inside the semicircle black. Leave to dry. Form the hat into a cone and glue the straight edges together.

3 Punch a hole at either side of the hat. Cut the length of ribbon in half and poke through the holes. Knot the ends of the ribbon over the holes.

4 To make the body shape, cut a length of card large enough to wrap around your body. Cut out ovals for armholes at each side of the card 5cm (2in) below the upper edge. Paint the card blue and leave to dry. Try on the costume and ask a friend to help you overlap the edges at the back and fasten them with stick-on Velcro.

MYTHICAL MERMAID

Choose green or blue shiny fabric to make this exotic mermaid costume. Decorate the wig and the costume with shells collected from the beach, or buy gold-coloured shells from a craft shop or department store. Sew sequins on to your leggings to give the effect of shimmering fish scales. The tail is cleverly elasticated at the knees to allow you to walk about!

1 To make the wig, cut the legs off the pair of tights. Matching the seams together, stitch across the cut edge in a curve to make a skull cap. Turn the cap right side out.

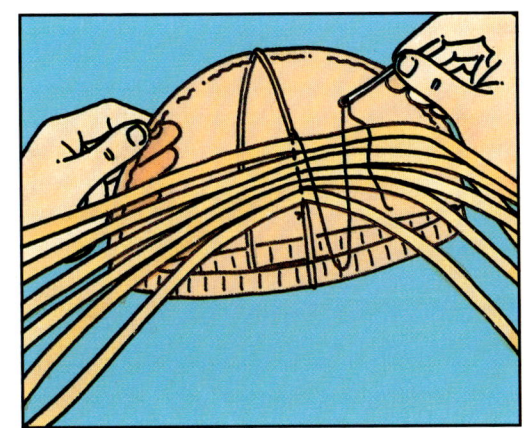

2 Cut lots of 110cm (43in) lengths of wool. Fold the lengths of wool in half and sew the centre of each piece to the centre seam of the skull cap. Do this until the skull cap is completely covered.

3 Now try on the wig, but you must protect your hair first with the shower cap or swimming hat. Lift up sections of the wool close to the stitching and glue to the skull cap. Glue shells to the wig while you are still wearing it. Ask an adult to help you do this. (Continued on the next page.)

(Continued on the next page.)

YOU WILL NEED

A pair of blue leggings
1m 10cm (1¼yd) of shiny fabric
Shells
Fine ribbon
2m 40cm (2½yd) of elastic
A pair of old tights
Speckled wool
Large sequins
Old shower cap or swimming hat
All-purpose glue
Scissors and pinking shears
Needle and thread
A safety pin

4 For the bikini top, cut a strip of shiny fabric 15cm (6in) wide and 81cm (32in) long. Sew the ends together.

5 Now make a channel on both long edges of the bikini top (see page 9). Thread both channels with elastic. Try on the bikini top and adjust the elastic to fit. Sew the ends of the elastic together. Tie a ribbon bow around the centre of the bikini top.

6 To make the tail, you will first need to make a full-size paper pattern following the diagram on page 87. To find out how to do this and how to cut out the pattern read the instructions on page 8. Now cut out two tail shapes from the shiny fabric using pinking shears. Sew the tail shapes together along the side seams using running stitch (see page 8).

7 Make a channel on the straight top edge of the tail in the same way as you did when making the bikini top. Thread the channel with elastic. Try on the tail and pull the ends of the elastic so that the tail fits comfortably under your knees. Sew the ends of the elastic together.

8 To finish, sew sequins to the leggings and glue shells to the bikini top and the tail.

SLEEPY HEAD

An old pair of pyjamas is the main ingredient for this bedtime outfit. Make a nightcap from the pyjama trousers and take your favourite teddy bear or a candleholder along to the party to complete the sleepy head costume.

1 Try on the pyjama top. If the sleeves are too long cut off the bottoms. Fold under the raw edges and stitch in place.

2 To make the nightcap, cut along the inside leg seams on the trouser legs and lay open the fabric. Use the hemmed bottom edge of the trouser legs as the bottom edge of your nightcap. Cut two triangles from the legs, 42cm (16½in) wide across the bottom edge by 42cm (16½in) along the slanted edges.

3 Pin the triangles together along the slanted edges on the wrong side of the fabric. Sew the triangles together and turn the hat to the right side.

4 To finish sew a tassel to the top of the hat. Wear the hat with the hemmed edge rolled up.

YOU WILL NEED
An old pair of adult's pyjamas
A white tassel
Needle and thread
Scissors and pins
A teddy bear
A pair of furry slippers
A candleholder and candle

LADY LUCK

Choose your own lucky card for this very simple playing card outfit. Add red ribbon for a red card, black ribbon for a black one. A leotard or swimming costume is all that you need to wear under the card costume. Make a dice hat to complete the outfit.

YOU WILL NEED
A leotard or swimming costume
2 large sheets of white card
Red sticky-backed plastic
5m (5½yd) of red ribbon
A square box about 14cm (5½in) wide
Round white stickers
Black poster paint and paintbrush
Scrap card and pencil
Hat elastic
Scissors and stapler

1 Cut the sheets of card to size using the photograph as a guide. Now cut away the corners of the cards in a curve. Draw the shapes you would like to decorate your cards with on to scrap card. Cut out the shapes to use as patterns.

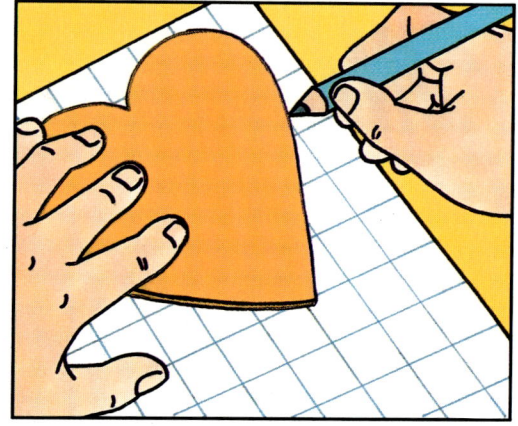

2 Place the patterns face down on to the back of the sticky-backed plastic and draw around them. Cut out the shapes. Peel the backing paper off the sticky-backed plastic and carefully stick the shapes in position on the playing cards.

3 Cut the ribbon into eight equal pieces. Staple two pieces to the top of each card 10cm (4in) in from each side. Staple a piece of ribbon to both sides of each card 25cm (10in) below the top edge. Wear the cards with the ribbons tied in a bow on your shoulders and under your arms.

4 To make the dice hat, paint the box black and leave to dry. Stick round white stickers to the sides. Make a hole at each side of the box and thread with hat elastic. Knot the ends of the elastic together.

LEAPING FROG

A green body stocking or a T-shirt and a pair of tights are the main items for this clever froggy outfit. The webbed hands and feet are cut from PVC while the flying insect is just a pipe cleaner twisted around a sweet paper. Make the mask extra special by adding joggle eyes.

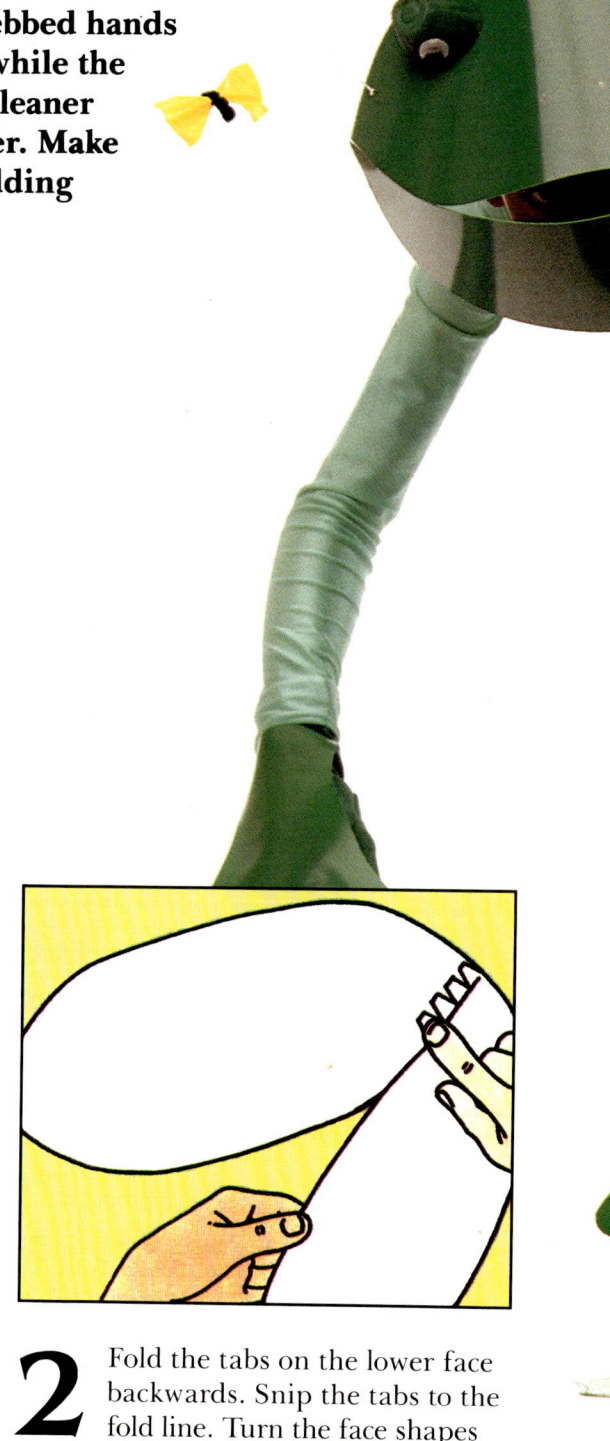

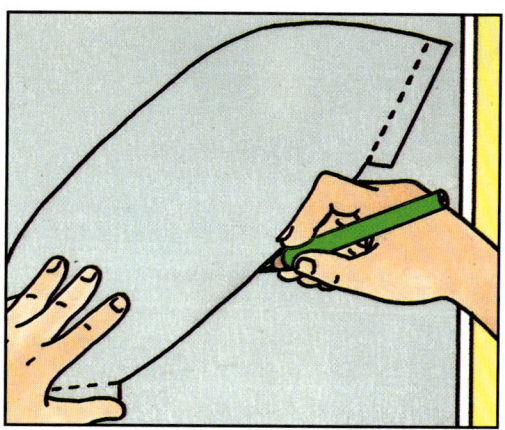

1 To make the mask, trace the upper and lower face patterns on pages 88 and 89 with a pencil. Lay the tracings face down on to the back of the green card. Rub over the outlines with a pencil. The patterns will appear on the card; cut out.

2 Fold the tabs on the lower face backwards. Snip the tabs to the fold line. Turn the face shapes over so that the back of the card is facing you. Starting at the corners, glue the tabs under the lower edge of the upper face.

3 Make a hole at the dots on the upper face and thread with hat elastic. Knot the ends over the holes. Cut two sections from the egg carton. Paint the egg sections green and, when dry, glue a joggle eye to each one. Glue the egg sections to the upper face. Draw nostrils with a black felt-tip pen on to the upper face. (Continued on the next page.)

YOU WILL NEED
A green body stocking and a pair of green gloves
Green and white card
Green paint and paintbrush
50cm (20in) of green PVC 90cm (36in) wide
Cardboard egg carton
Black pipe-cleaner
Black felt-tip pen
80cm (30in) of hat elastic
30cm (12in) of elastic 13mm (½in) wide
Fine wire and a sweet paper
Red paper and scissors
All-purpose glue and tape

SAFETY TIP: *Make sure an adult helps you when using wire.*

4 To make the tongue, cut two strips of red paper 21 x 2cm (8 x 1in). Glue fine wire down the middle of one strip. Glue the strips together, sandwiching the wire. Cut one end of the tongue into a 'V' shape and glue the other end inside the mouth.

5 For the fly, cut a piece of black pipe-cleaner 8cm (3in) long and bend in half. Twist a sweet paper at the centre and slip it between the pipe-cleaner halves. Twist the ends of the pipe-cleaner together as shown. Twist a length of fine wire around the pipe-cleaner and tape the other end to the mask.

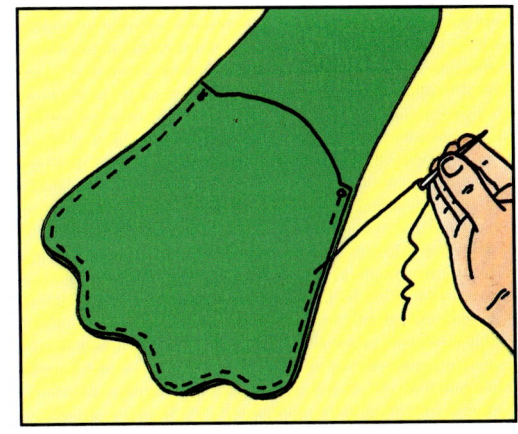

8 Stitch the shoe uppers to the PVC shoe soles, carefully matching the dots shown on the patterns. To finish, glue the card soles under the PVC soles.

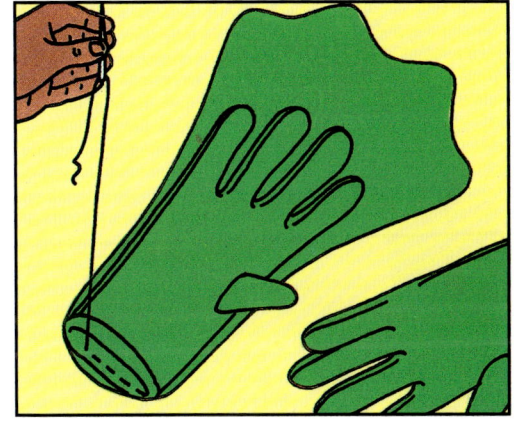

9 For the webbed hands, trace the pattern on page 92 and cut out. Tape the pattern on to a double layer of PVC and cut out two hand shapes. Sew the hands to the back of the gloves.

6 To make the webbed shoes, trace the upper and sole patterns on pages 90 and 91. Lay the shoe sole pattern face down on to white card and rub over the outline with a pencil. The pattern will appear on the card; cut out. Now lay the shape back on to the card, draw around it and cut out another shoe sole. Lay one of the soles on to a double layer of green PVC and keep in place with sticky tape. Cut out two PVC soles.

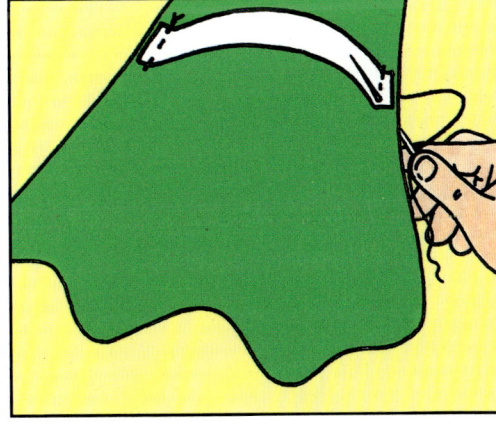

7 Cut two 11.5cm (4½in) lengths of wide elastic. Stitch each end to the PVC soles at the dots shown on the pattern. Wear the shoes with the elastic over your feet. Now cut out the tracing for the webbed shoe upper. Tape it to a double layer of green PVC and cut out two PVC shoe uppers.

VAMPIRE

Large squares of black and red satin stitched together make a splendid cloak for this stunning outfit. You will probably have a plain white shirt and black or dark grey trousers to dress up with a ribbon sash. Make a black top hat and wear a pair of fangs for added effect.

1 To make the cloak, cut a 120cm (47in) square of black and red satin. Pin the squares together, right sides in. Sew running stitch (see page 8), along the four edges leaving a gap in one edge so you can turn the cloak right side out. Turn the cloak to the right side and sew across the gap. Sew a row of running stitch through both pieces of fabric 9cm (3½ in) below one edge.

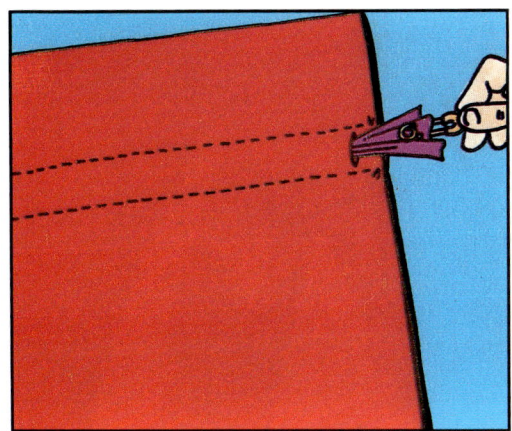

YOU WILL NEED
Old white shirt, black
 trousers and shoes
1m 30cm (1½yd) of black satin
 150cm (60in) wide
1m 30cm (1½yd) of red satin
 150cm (60in) wide
3m (3¼yd) of wide mauve
 ribbon
60cm (24in) of wide black
 ribbon
Black card and glue
Plastic fangs (from joke shop)
Needle and thread
Scissors and pencil

2 Sew another row of stitches 2.5cm (1in) below the first row to make a channel. Carefully unpick a few of the stitches in the sides of the cloak at each end of the channel. Cut a piece of mauve ribbon 160cm (63in) long. Attach a safety pin to one end thread it through the channel. Feel for the pin through the fabric and ease it through the channel.

3 To make the hat, cut a strip of black card 55cm (22in) long by 20cm (8in) wide. Draw a line 1.5cm (⅝in) above one long edge. Fold the card along the line and cut tabs along the edge. Form the strip into a tube shape and glue the long edges together. This is the crown of the hat.

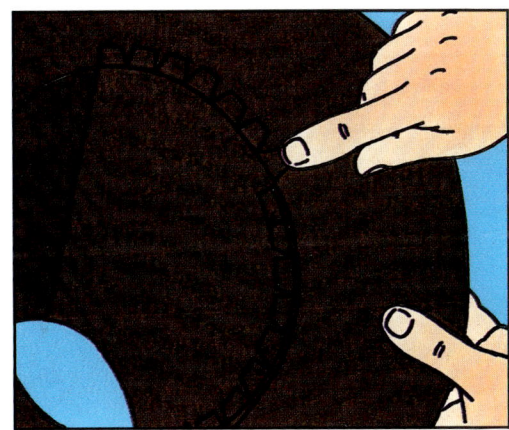

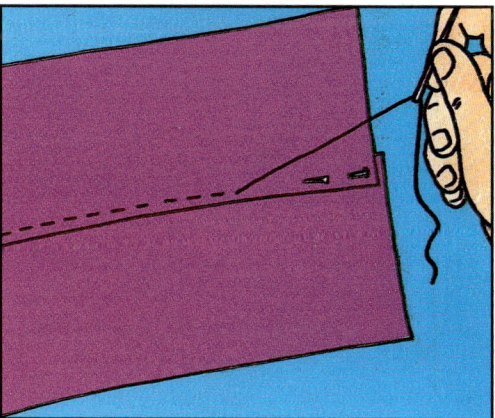

4 For the brim, cut out a circle of black card with a diameter of 30cm (12in). Stand the straight edge of the crown in the centre of the circle and draw round it. Cut out the circle. Slip the hat brim over the crown and glue the snipped edge under the brim. Glue black ribbon around the hat for a hatband.

5 Cut the remaining piece of mauve ribbon in half length-wise to make a sash. Overlap the long edges and stitch together. To finish, make a hem at each end (see page 9). Tie the sash around your waist.

MENACING MONSTER

Make this monster costume as fearsome as possible by sewing pieces of bubble wrap to the body stocking to look like scales and making bubble wrap humps to attach to the back. If you don't have a body stocking, a T-shirt and a pair of leggings or tights would be just as good.

1 To make the mask, trace the upper and lower face patterns on pages 88 and 89 with a pencil. Lay the tracings face down on to the back of the purple card and rub over the outlines with a pencil. The patterns will appear on the card; cut out. Fold the tabs on the lower face backwards. Snip the tabs to the fold lines.

2 Turn the face shapes over so the back of the card is facing you. Starting at the corners, glue the tabs under the lower edge of the upper face. Make a hole at the dots on the upper face and thread with hat elastic. Knot the elastic over the holes. Glue the eyes to the upper face.

3 Put some green paint into a shallow dish. Using a sponge, dab paint on to pieces of bubble wrap and leave to dry. Cut out shapes from the bubble wrap and glue to the mask. Cut out some more shapes to attach to the body stocking later.

4 To make the humps, cut two 15cm (6in) diameter circles from bubble wrap. Cut the circles in half and staple the half circles together as shown. Leave the bottom edge open. Screw up some tissue paper and stuff it into the humps.

5 Try on the body stocking and fix safety pins to the places where you want to attach the pieces of bubble wrap and the humps. Ask an adult to help you do this. Take off the body stocking. Catch the bubble wrap pieces and the humps to the body stocking with a few stitches. Paint a piece of scrap card green and cut six triangles for claws. Sew or glue three claws to the toe of each sock.

YOU WILL NEED
A purple body stocking and a pair of purple socks
Purple card and bubble wrap
Green poster paint and brush
Shallow dish and sponge
80cm (32in) of hat elastic
2 funny fake eyes (from toy shops)
Green tissue paper
All-purpose glue
Tracing paper and pencil
Needle and thread
Scissors and stapler

CRAZY CLOWN

You'll be the centre of attention in this colourful clown costume. Decorate the shirt with glitter paints and make braces from bright red ribbon. To make the waist of the trousers stand out, replace the elastic in the waistband with boning which is available from department stores. To complete your outfit make a glittery hat, a pair of extra large shoes and a big bow-tie.

YOU WILL NEED
A pair of old tracksuit trousers
An adult's old shirt
Yellow card
1m (40in) of plastic boning
2m 30cm (2½ yd) of
   wide ribbon
40cm (16in) of yellow PVC
   90cm (36in) wide
30cm (12in) of elastic
   13mm (½in) wide
2m (2¼ yd) of hat elastic
Red metallic crêpe paper

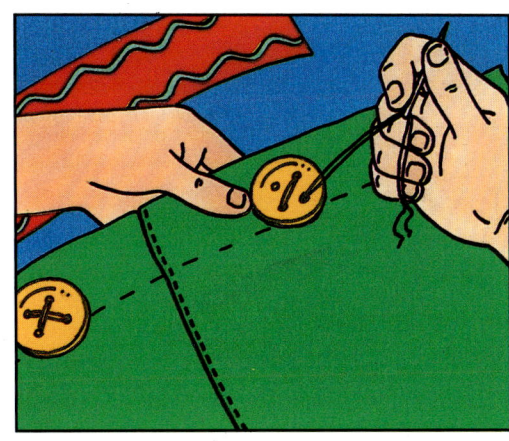

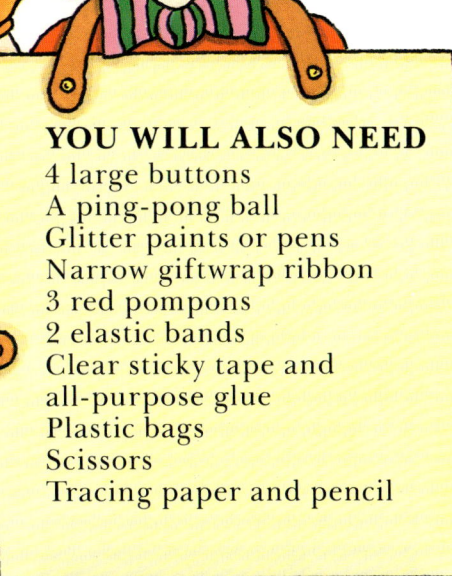

(Continued on the next page.)

1 Cut the cuffs off the shirt sleeves. Slip a plastic bag into the end of each sleeve and decorate the bottom of the sleeves with glitter paints. Wear the shirt with elastic bands slipped over the wrists to gather in the sleeves.

3 To make the braces, cut the ribbon in half and decorate with glitter paints. Sew two buttons to the front of the trousers and two to the back 7.5cm (3in) either side of the front and back seams. Cut a slit in one end of the ribbon braces and fasten on to the buttons on the back of the trousers.

YOU WILL ALSO NEED
4 large buttons
A ping-pong ball
Glitter paints or pens
Narrow giftwrap ribbon
3 red pompons
2 elastic bands
Clear sticky tape and all-purpose glue
Plastic bags
Scissors
Tracing paper and pencil

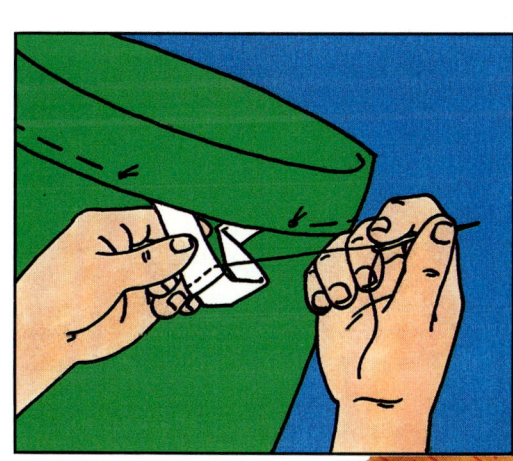

2 Carefully unpick a few stitches on the waistband of the trousers and pull out the elastic. Push the boning into the waistband channel until it comes out the other end. Sew the ends of the boning together.

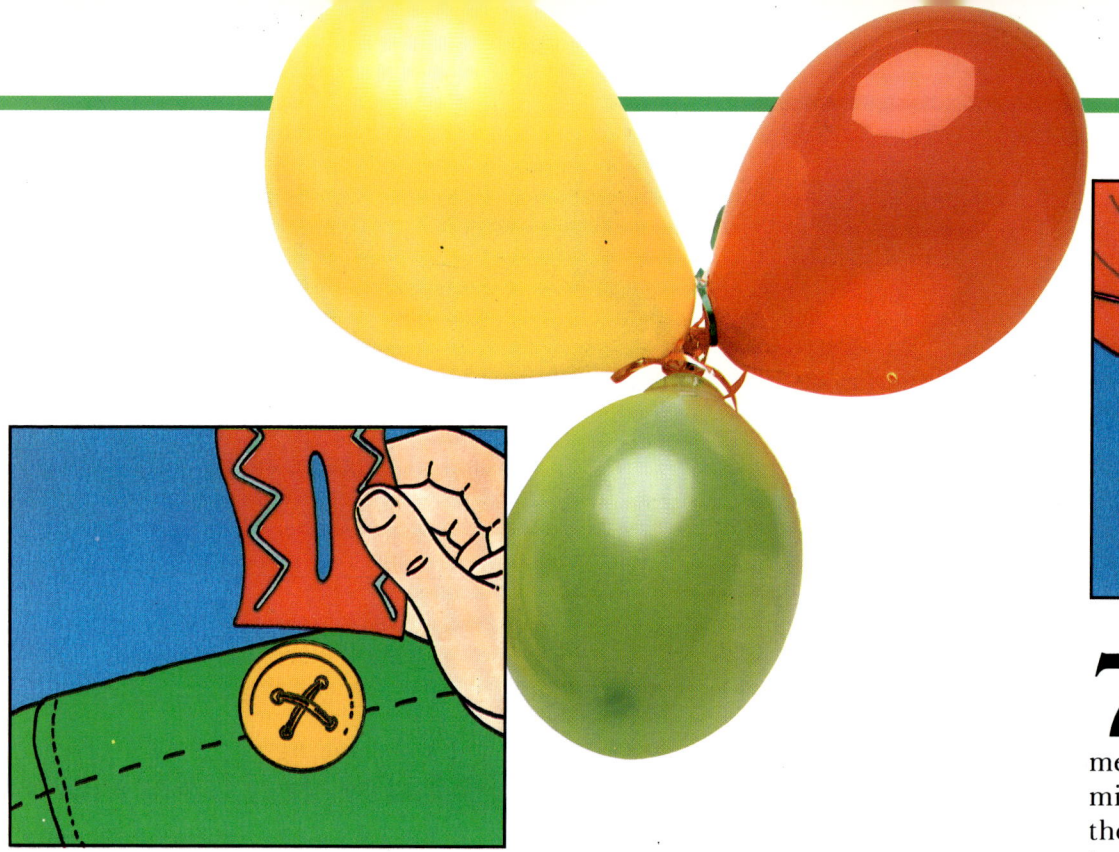

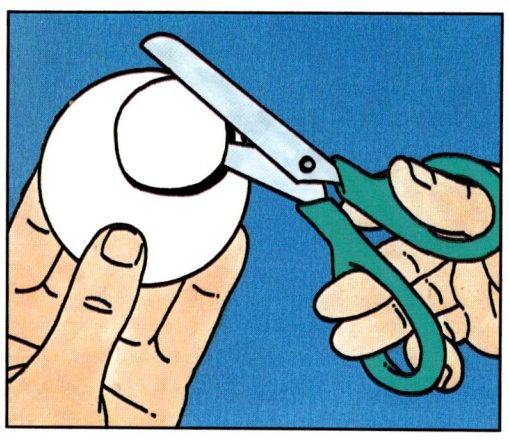

4 Try the trousers on and pull the braces over your shoulders. Cut slits in the other ends of the braces and fasten to the front buttons.

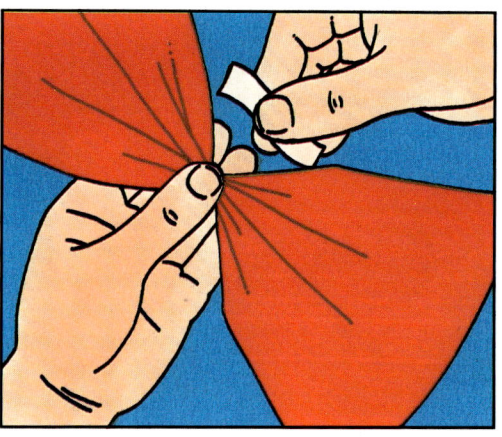

5 For the nose, cut a hole in the ping-pong ball large enough to fit over your nose. Paint the ball with glitter paint and leave to dry. Make a hole at each side of the ball and thread with hat elastic. Knot the elastic at the back of your head.

6 Cut a rectangle of metallic crêpe paper 30 x 16cm (12 x 6¼in) for the bow-tie and two rectangles 20 x 12.5cm (8 x 5in) for the shoe bows. Squeeze the rectangles in the middle to make bows and bind with sticky tape. Decorate the bows with glitter paints.

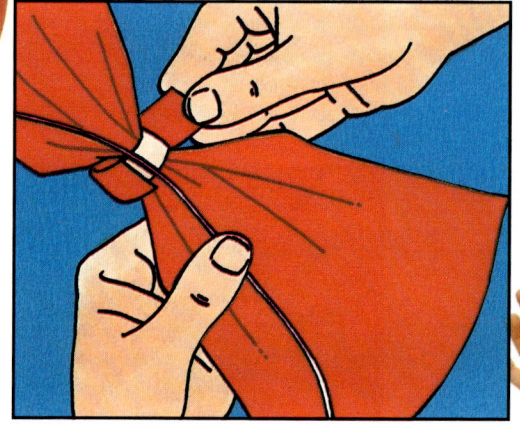

7 Place a length of hat elastic across the back of the bow-tie. Wrap a narrow strip of metallic crêpe paper around the middle and secure with glue. Knot the ends of the elastic together at the back of your neck.

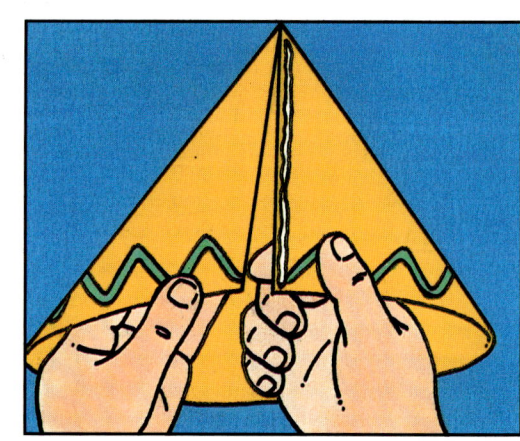

8 Trace the hat pattern on pages 94 and 95, and lay it face down on to yellow card. Rub over the outline with a pencil. The pattern will appear on the card; cut out. Decorate with glitter paints. Overlap the straight edges and glue together. Decorate with pompons. Make a hole at each side of the hat and thread with hat elastic. Glue giftwrap ribbon inside the hat.

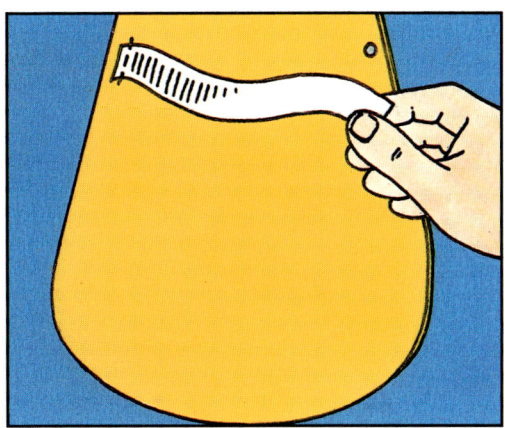

10 Cut two 11.5cm (4½in) lengths of wide elastic. Stitch each end to the PVC soles at the dots shown on the pattern. Wear the shoes with the elastic over your feet. Now cut out the tracing for the shoe upper. Tape it on to a double layer of yellow PVC and cut out two shoe uppers.

9 To make the shoes, trace the upper and sole patterns on pages 93 and 94. Lay the shoe sole tracing face down on to card and rub over the outline with a pencil. The pattern will appear on the card; cut out. Now lay the shape back on to the card, draw around it and cut out another shoe sole. Lay one of the soles on to a double layer of yellow PVC and keep in place with sticky tape. Cut out two PVC soles.

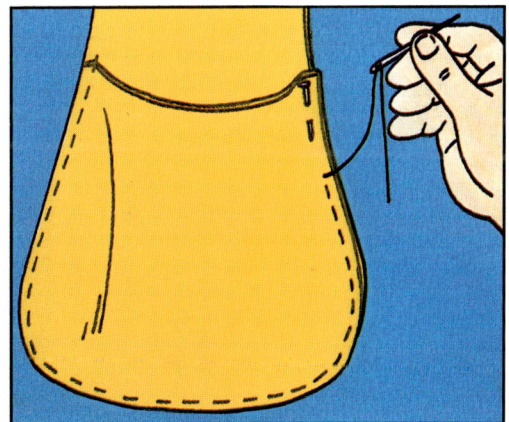

11 Stitch the uppers to the PVC soles, matching the soles to the uppers at the dots shown on the patterns. Glue the card soles under the PVC soles. Glue the shoe bows to the shoes.

CHRISTMAS TREE

Why go to a party as a Christmas fairy when you can dress up as the whole tree? The basic cape and skirt are made from green metallic crêpe paper gathered on to sticky-backed plastic waist and neck bands. Once you have made the tree-top hat you can trim the outfit with lots of baubles, tinsel and other decorations.

1 To make the waistband, cut a strip of sticky-backed plastic 4cm (1½in) wide and long enough to fit around your waist plus 5cm (2in). Cut another strip 40cm (15½in) long and 4cm (1½in) wide for the neckband. Stick double-sided tape along one long edge of the backing paper on the waistband and the neckband. Do not remove the backing paper on the sticky-backed plastic.

YOU WILL NEED
A green body stocking or
 a green T-shirt and tights
Green metallic crêpe paper
Thin card
Gold sticky-backed plastic
70cm (28in) of hat elastic
Lightweight Christmas garland
 and tree decorations
Stick-on Velcro
Double-sided sticky tape
 and clear sticky tape
Needle and thread
All-purpose glue
Scissors and tape measure
Tracing paper and pencil

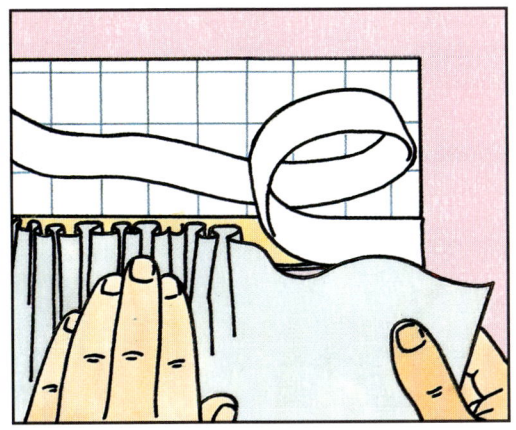

2 Cut two strips of metallic crêpe paper 180 x 30cm (70 x 12in). These are for the skirt and the cape. To make the skirt, gradually peel the backing paper off the double-sided tape on the waistband and stick the long edge of one strip of crêpe paper to the tape. Gather up the crêpe paper to fit. Fasten the ends of the waistband with Velcro. Join the cape to the neck-band in the same way.

3 For the hat, trace the pattern on pages 94 and 95. Lay the tracing face down on to thin card. Rub over the outline with a pencil. The pattern will appear on the card; cut out the shape. Glue metallic crêpe paper to the hat shape and trim the edges. Cut slits in the top of the hat as shown on the pattern. Form the hat into a cone, overlap the straight edges and glue together.

4 Pierce a hole at each side of the hat and thread with hat elastic. Knot the ends of the elastic over the holes. Stick gold sticky-backed plastic to both sides of a piece of card and cut out a star shape. Slot the star into the slit at the top of the hat. Glue a garland around the bottom of the hat.

5 Drape garlands around the skirt and cape and stitch in place. Sew tree decorations to the hat, skirt and cape. Stick tape over the stitching on the wrong side of the crêpe paper so that the paper doesn't tear. Wrap a length of garland around each wrist and ask a friend to stick the ends together with tape.

MORE COSTUME IDEAS

Once you have made some of the costumes featured in this book, why not try creating your own original outfits? On these pages we have suggested ways that you can adapt some of the costumes by using different coloured materials and adding matching accessories.

MOUSE

Nose made from a ping-pong ball painted black. Glue whiskers to the nose.

Pink and grey felt ears sewn on to a hairband

White body stocking or a pair of white leggings and a T-shirt.

White gloves

Tail made from a length of cord.

BLACK CAT Page 44

WICKED WITCH Page 50

WIZARD

Black felt hat decorated with stars and moons cut from yellow felt.

Green wool hair.

Green nightgown.

Black cloak decorated with stars and moons cut from yellow felt.

RABBIT

Pink and grey card ears glued to a hairband.

Nose made from a ping-pong ball painted black. Glue whiskers to the nose.

White card teeth.

White gloves

Grey body stocking or a pair of grey leggings and a T-shirt.

Fluffy tail made from cotton wool.

SOUTHERN BELLE Page 22

GYPSY PRINCESS

Curtain rings for earrings

White T-shirt

Shawl or pretty scarf

Green skirt made from plastic bin bags trimmed with gold braid.

PENCIL PERSON Page 52

FLOWER

FIREWORK

Card cone hat decorated with glitter pens.

Brightly-coloured crêpe paper petals attached to elastic.

Card body shape decorated with poster paints and glitter pens.

Green crêpe paper leaves glued to body shape.

Green card body shape for the stem.

Crêpe paper frill.

PATTERNS

The following pages show the patterns you will need to make many of the projects featured in the book. To find out how to copy a pattern follow the step-by-step instructions given for each project.

Some of the patterns are shown as diagrams with measurements so that you can draw the correct size pattern piece on to paper. To find out how to do this follow the instructions for Making a Paper Pattern on page 8.

The patterns have all been designed to fit an average 9-10 year old. Check that the measurements given with the patterns are correct for you before cutting out the fabric. If necessary change the size of the pattern pieces to fit.

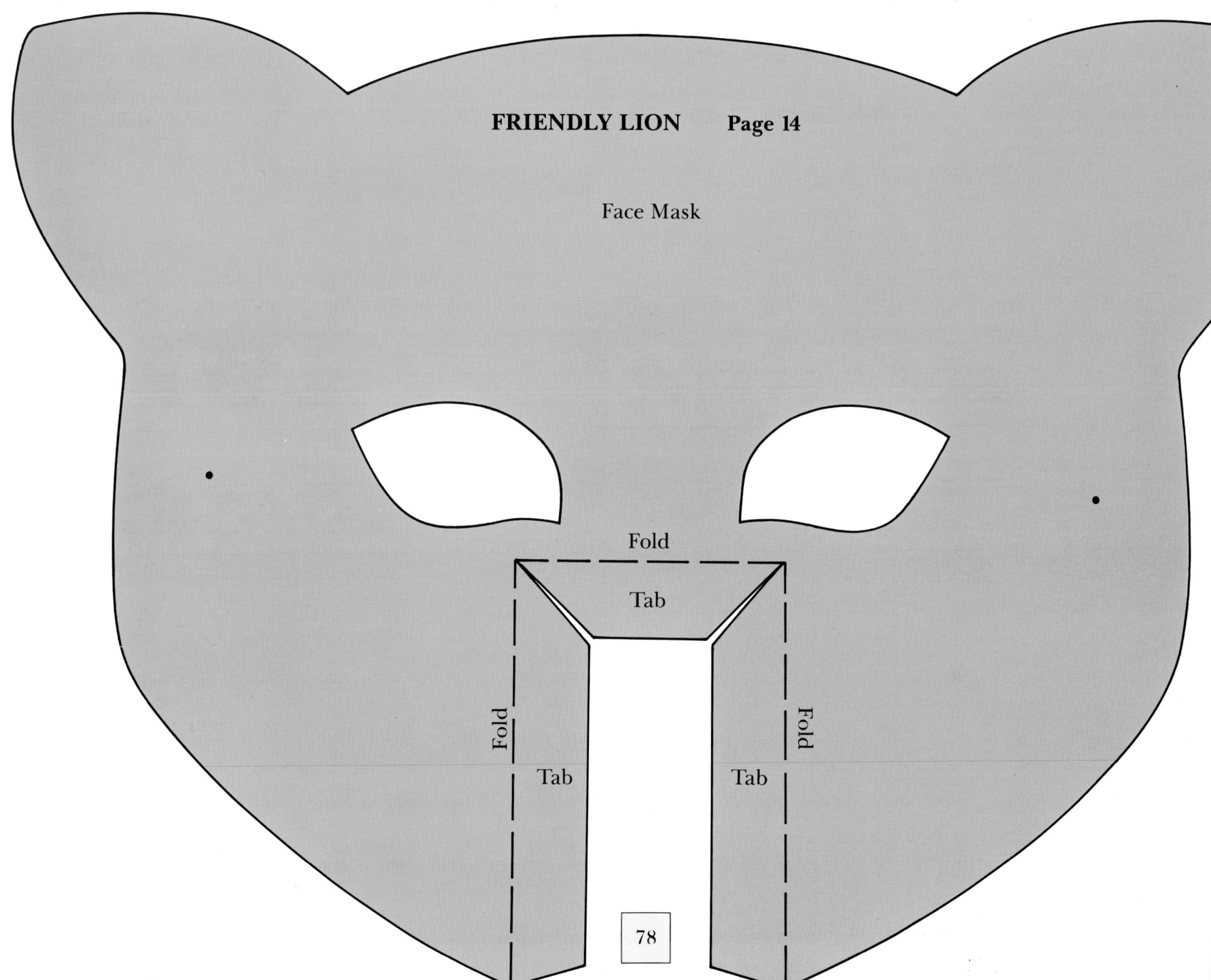

FRIENDLY LION   Page 14

Face Mask

Fold

Tab

Fold

Fold

Tab

Tab

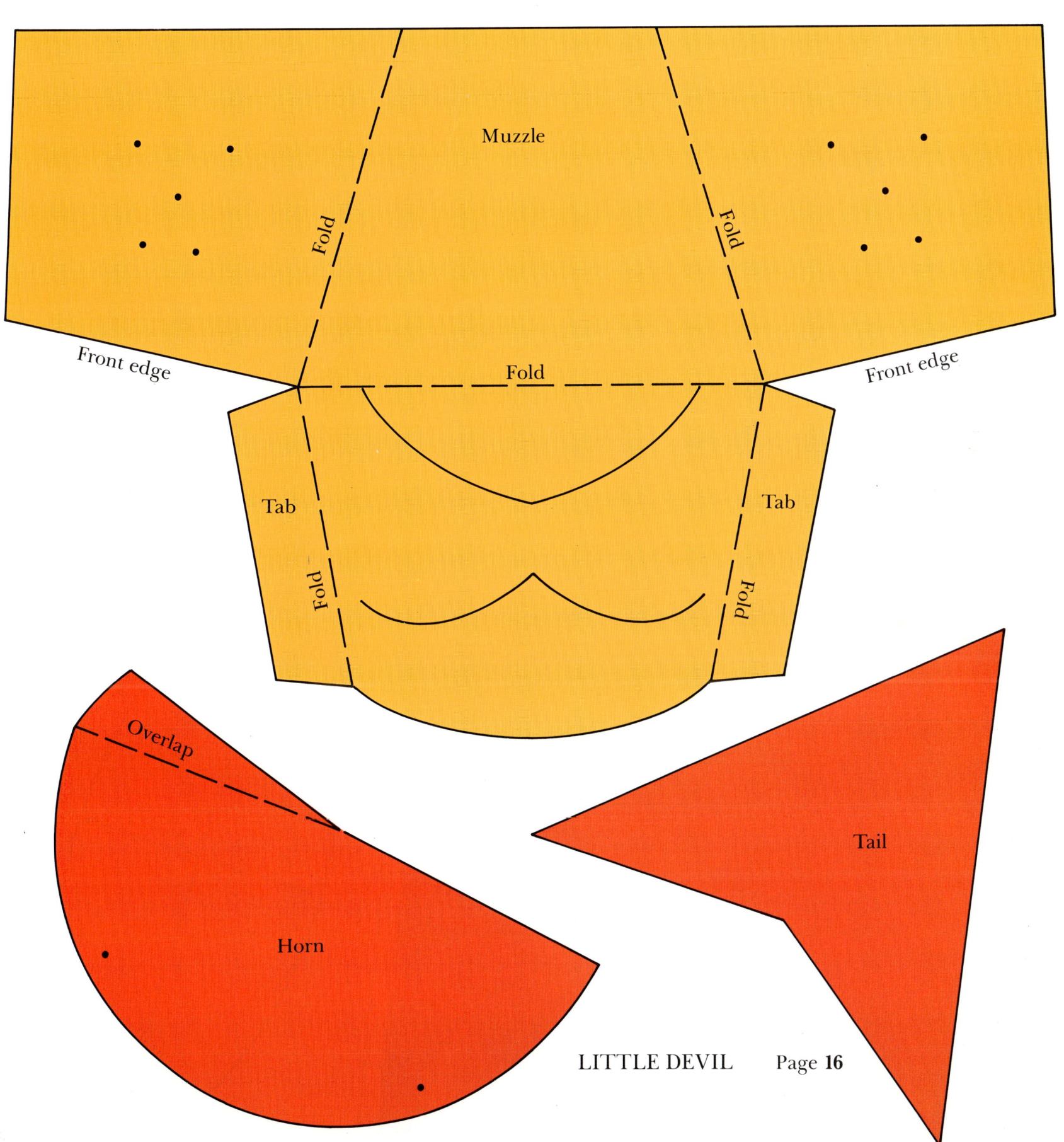

Muzzle

Fold

Fold

Front edge

Fold

Front edge

Fold

Tab

Fold

Tab

Fold

Overlap

Horn

Tail

LITTLE DEVIL   Page **16**

79

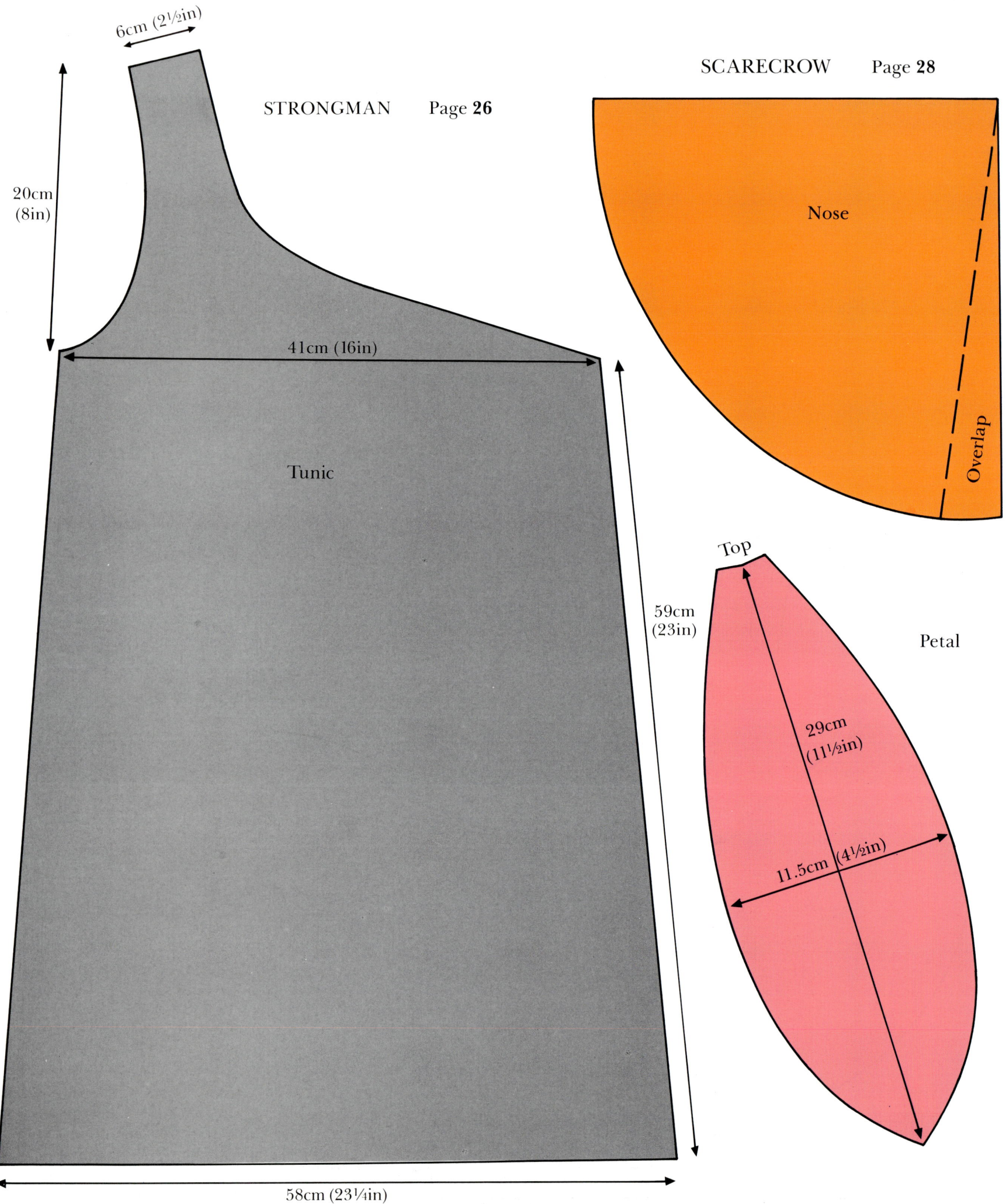

6cm (2½in)

STRONGMAN   Page **26**

SCARECROW   Page **28**

20cm (8in)

Nose

Overlap

41cm (16in)

Tunic

59cm (23in)

Top

Petal

29cm (11½in)

11.5cm (4½in)

58cm (23¼in)

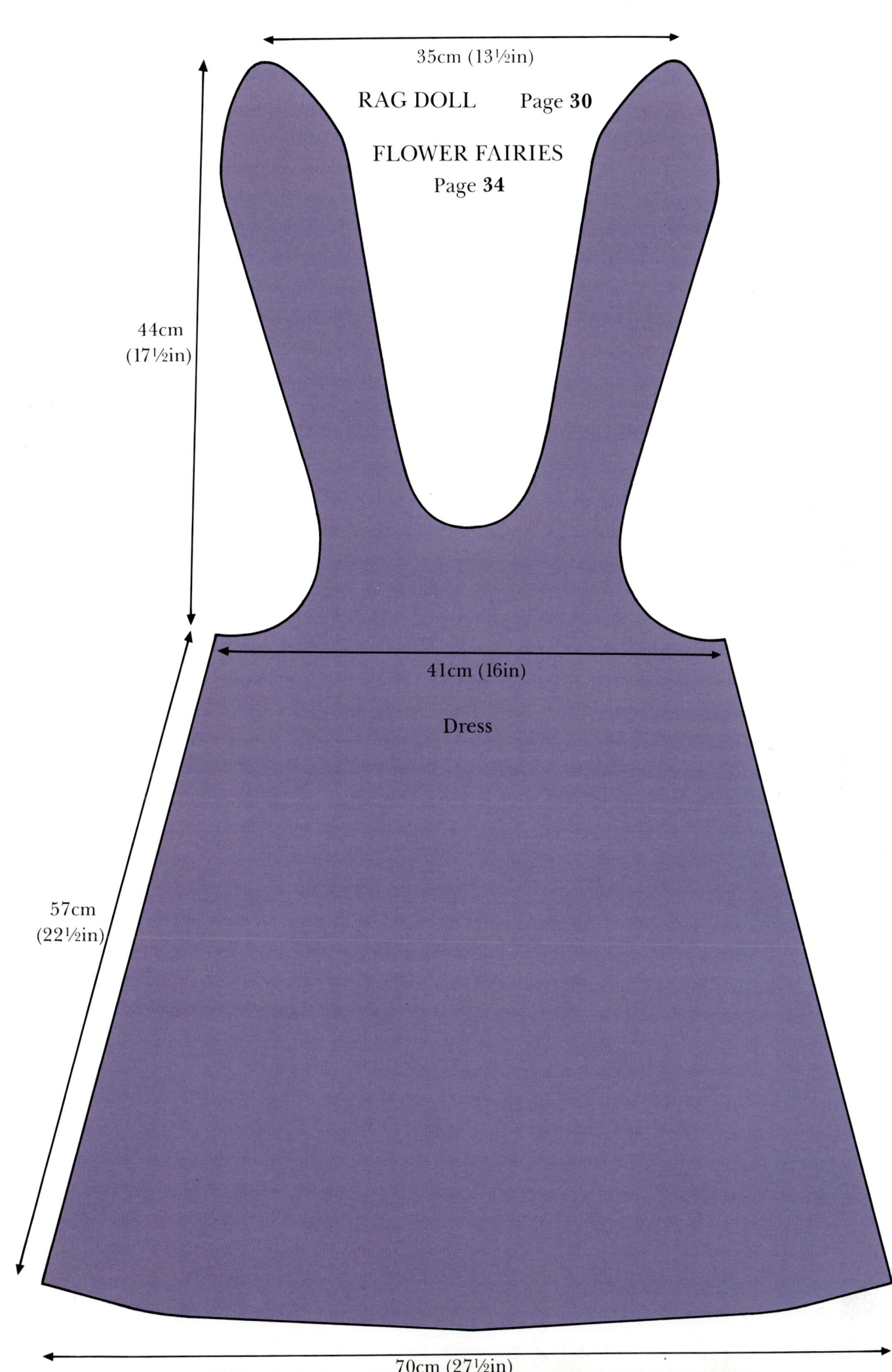

35cm (13½in)

RAG DOLL   Page **30**

FLOWER FAIRIES

Page **34**

44cm
(17½in)

41cm (16in)

Dress

57cm
(22½in)

70cm (27½in)

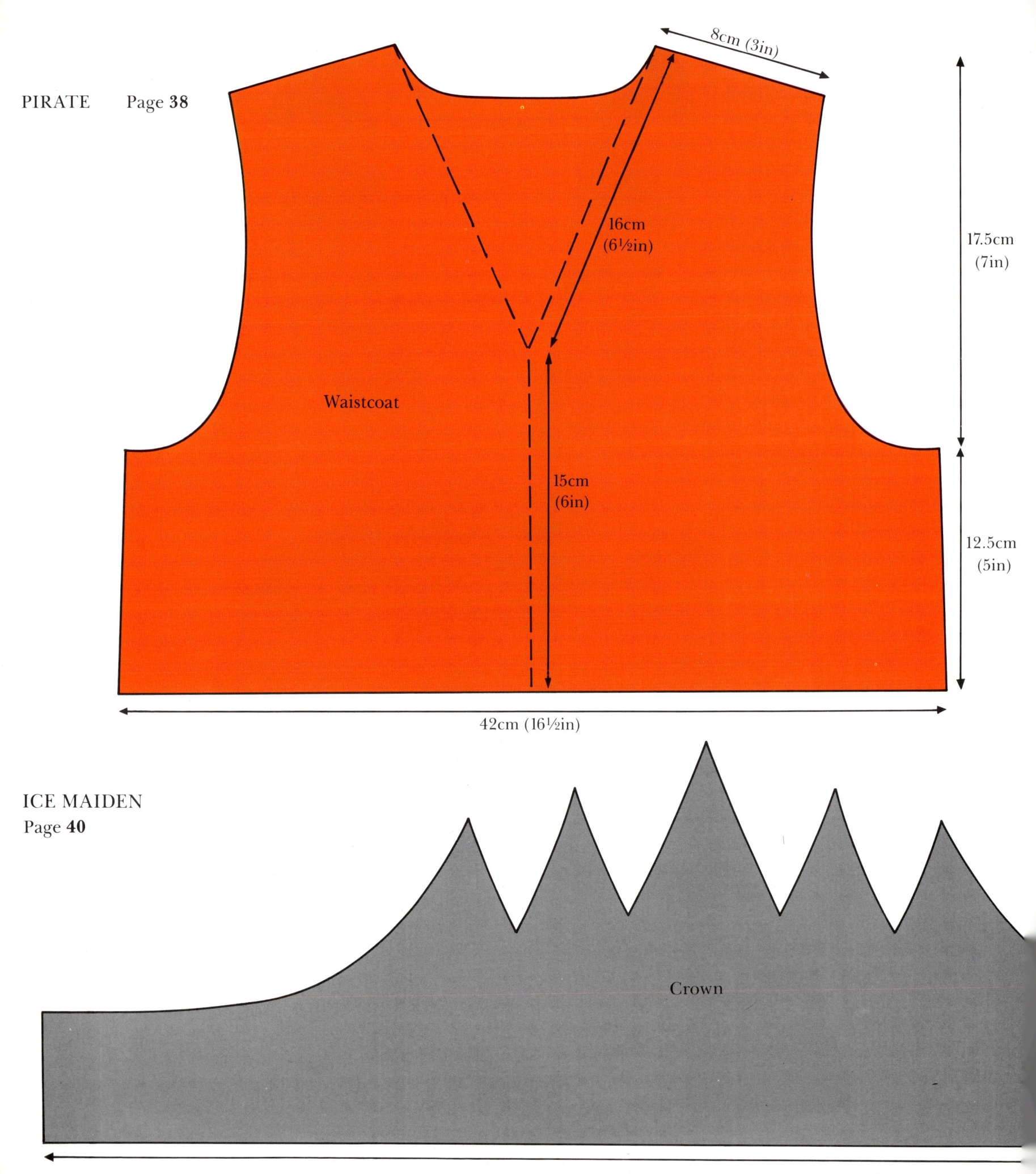

PIRATE   Page **38**

8cm (3in)

16cm
(6½in)

17.5cm
(7in)

Waistcoat

15cm
(6in)

12.5cm
(5in)

42cm (16½in)

ICE MAIDEN
Page **40**

Crown

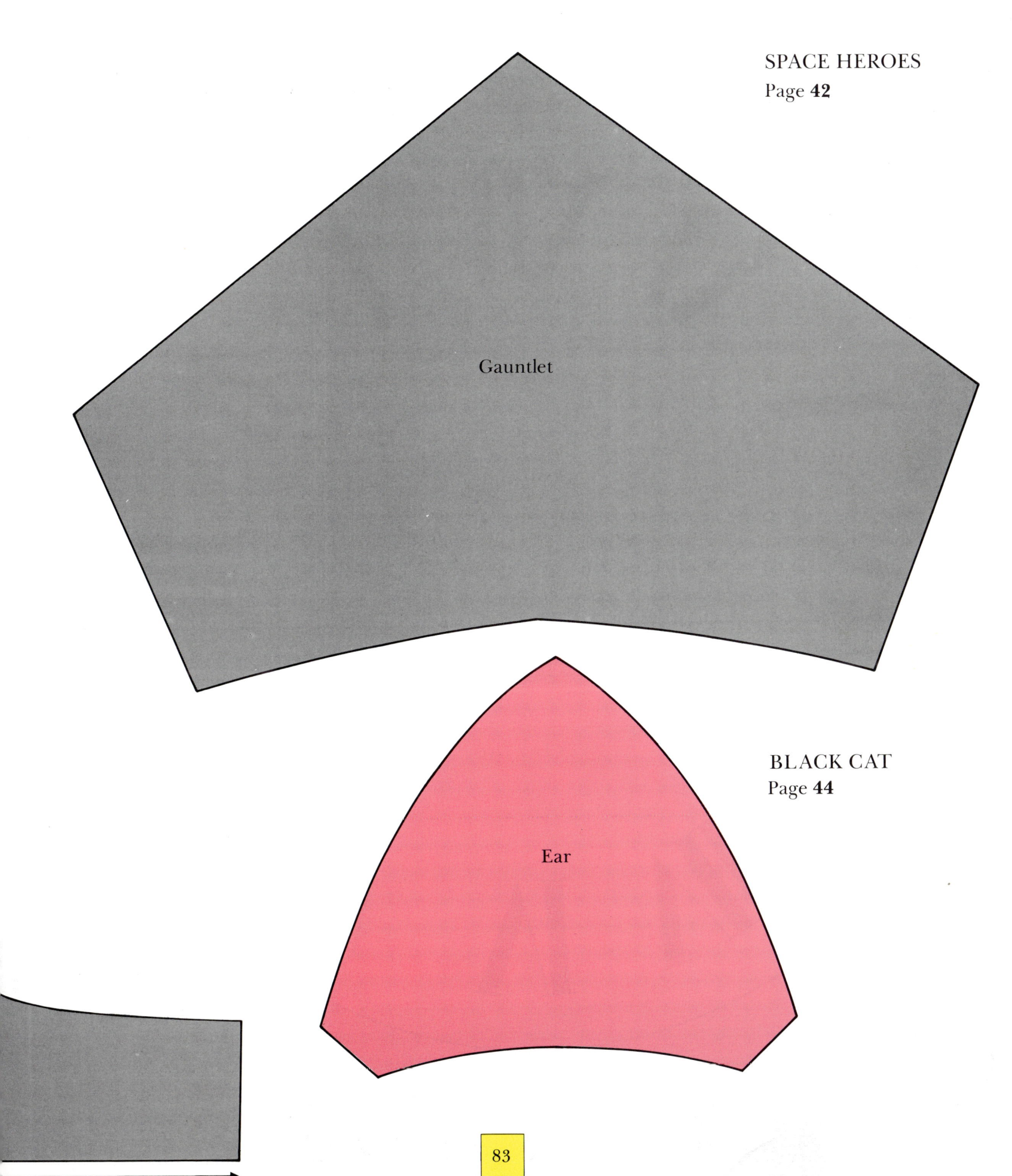

Gauntlet

BLACK CAT
Page **44**

Ear

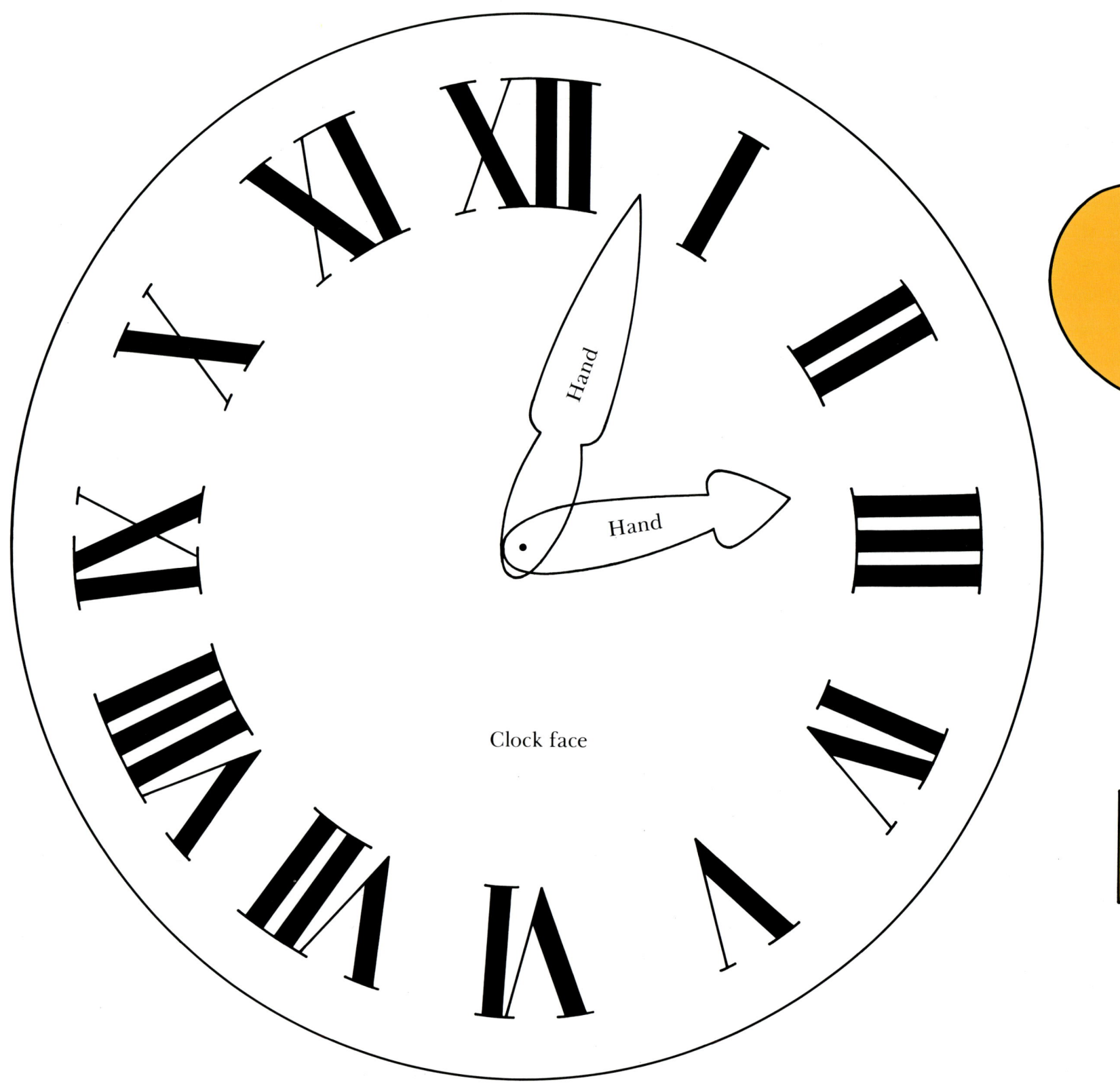

Hand

Hand

Clock face

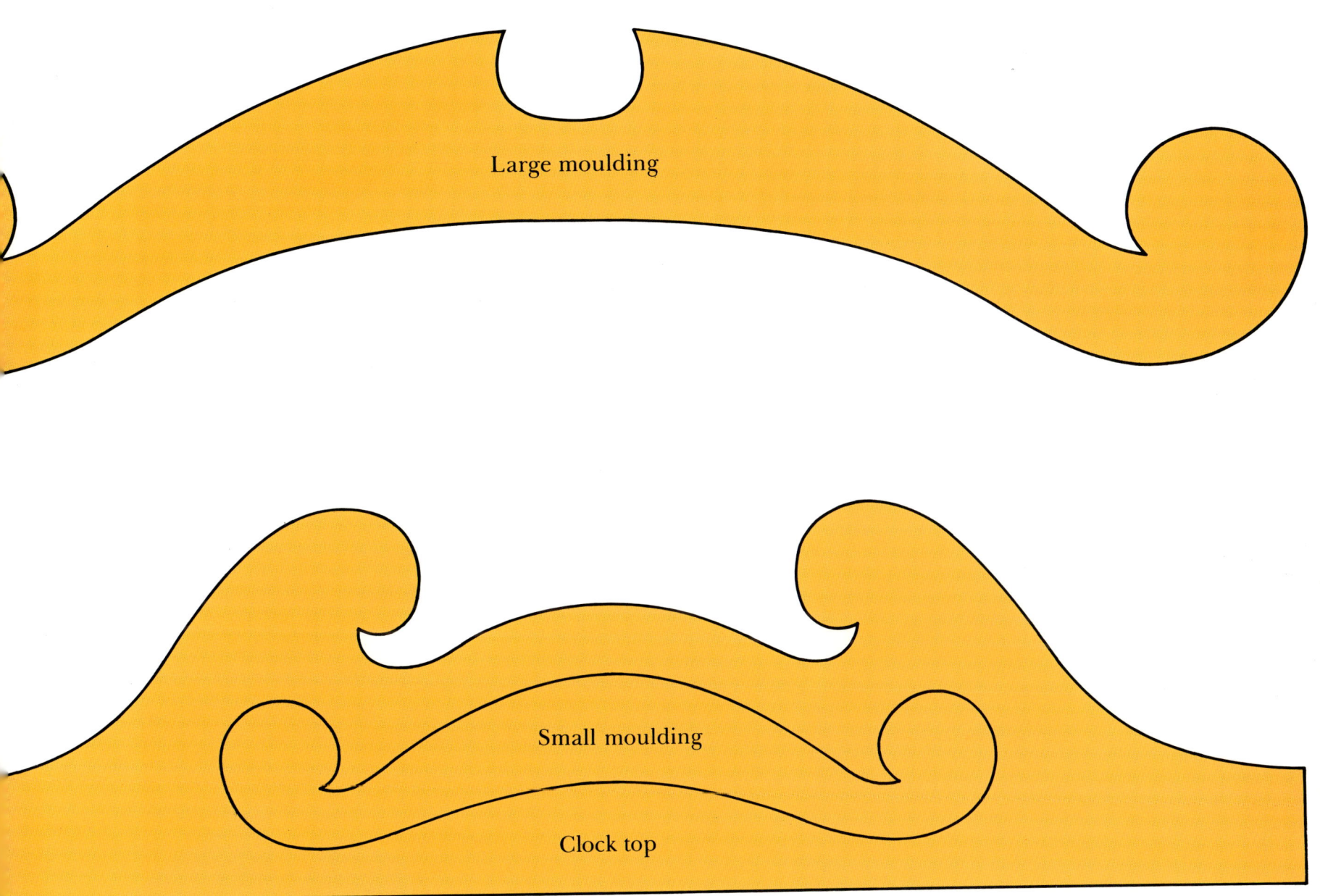

Large moulding

Small moulding

Clock top

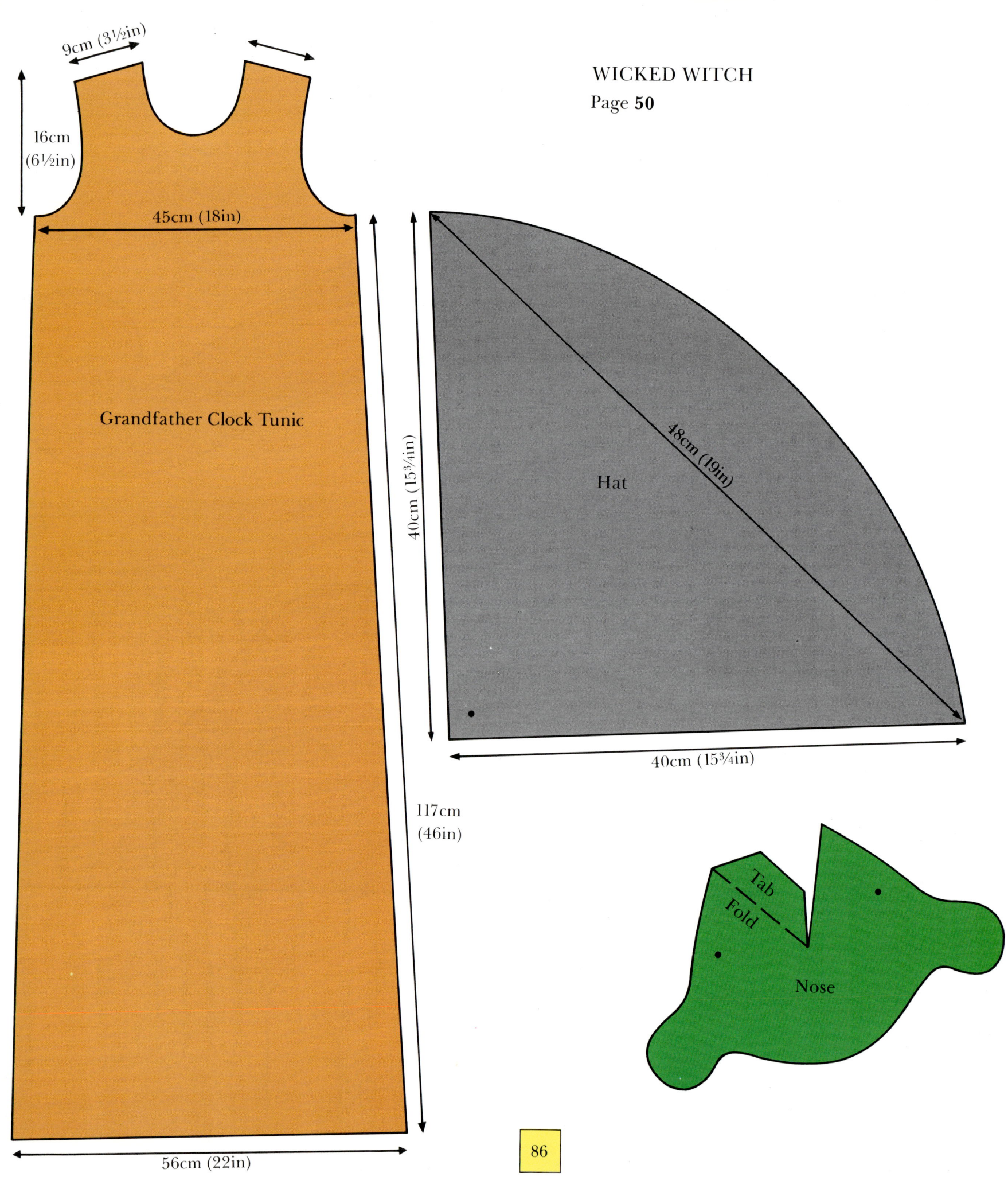

9cm (3½in)

16cm
(6½in)

45cm (18in)

Grandfather Clock Tunic

40cm (15¾in)

48cm (19in)

Hat

40cm (15¾in)

117cm
(46in)

56cm (22in)

Tab

Fold

Nose

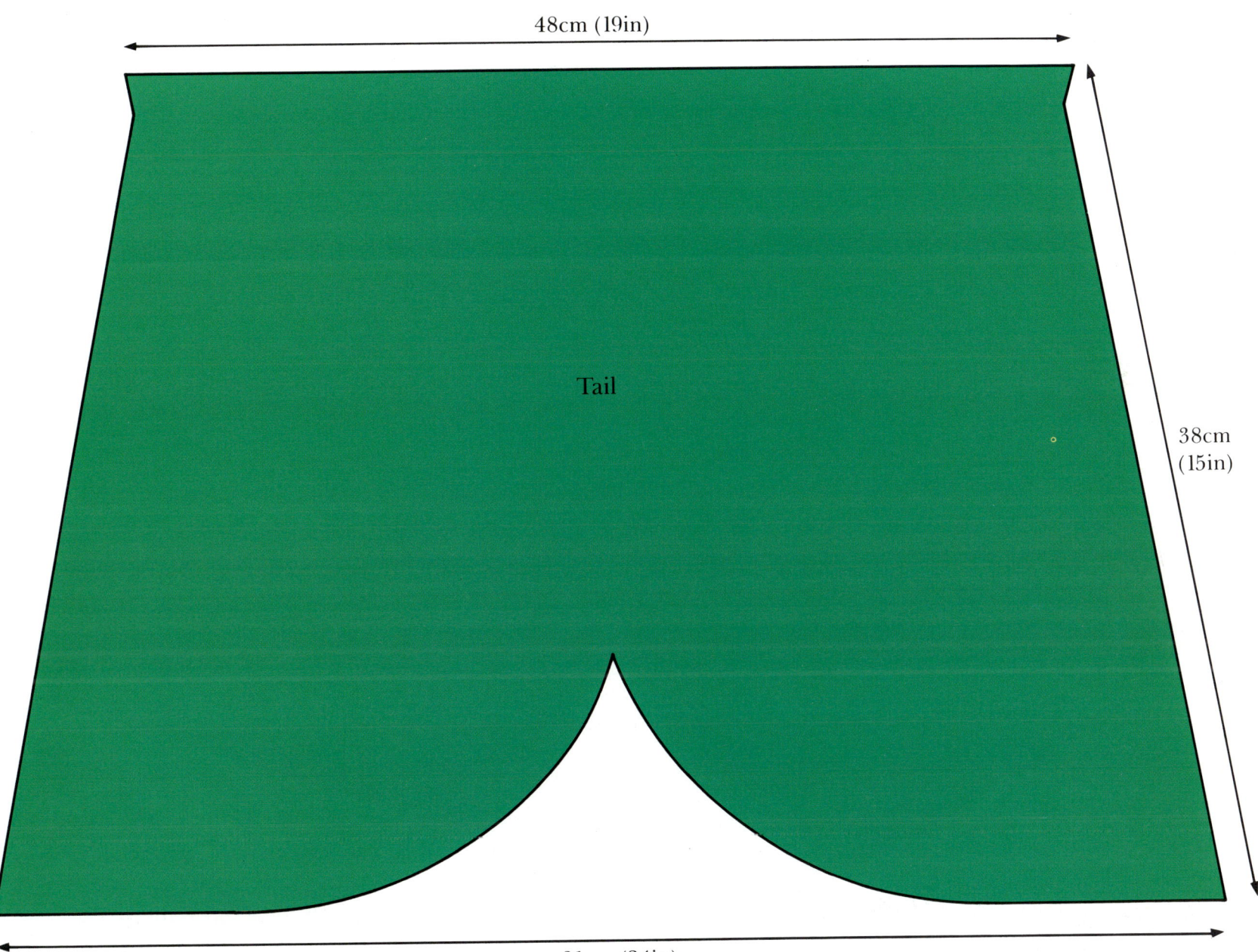

48cm (19in)

Tail

38cm (15in)

61cm (24in)

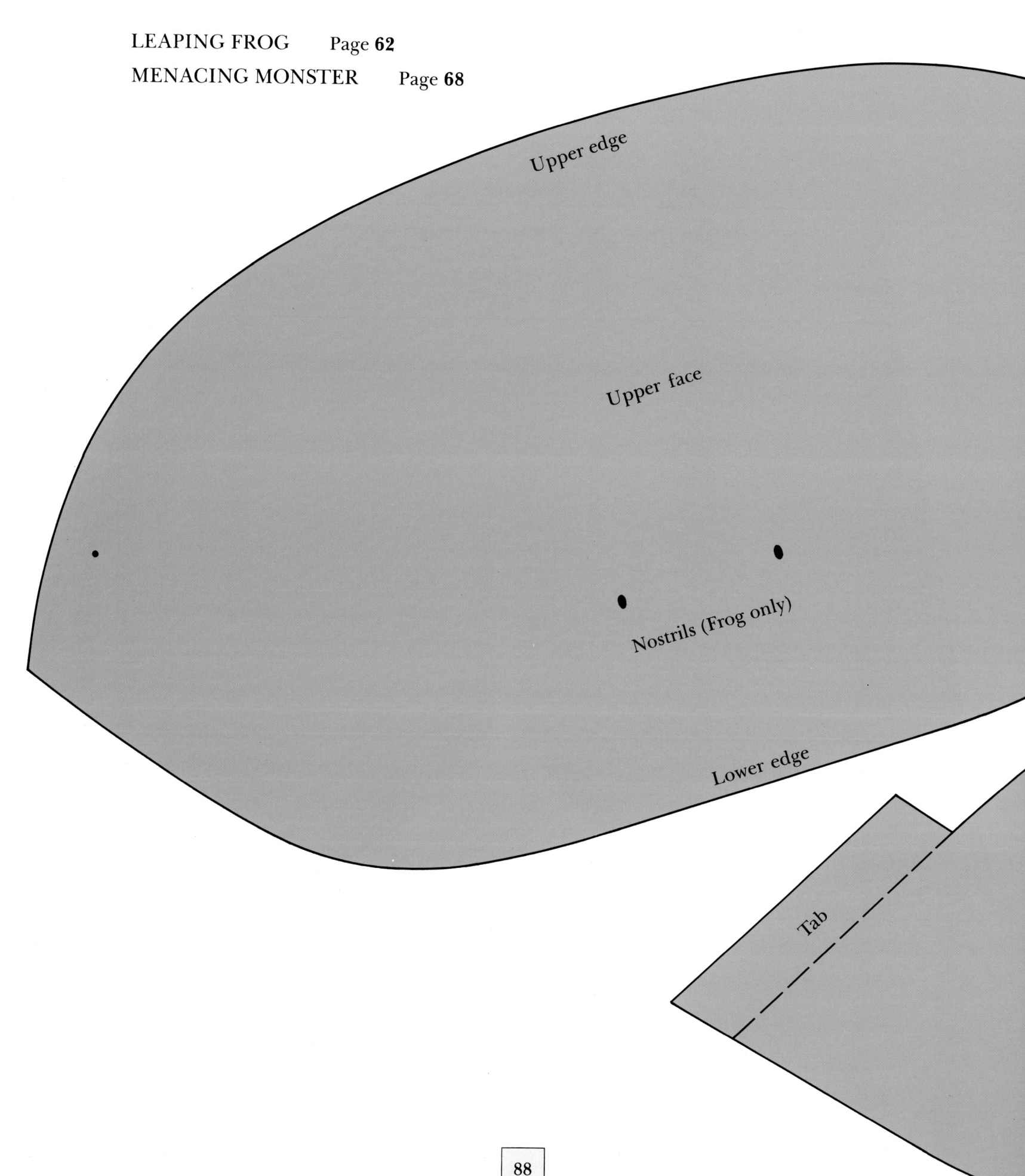

Upper edge

Upper face

Nostrils (Frog only)

Lower edge

Tab

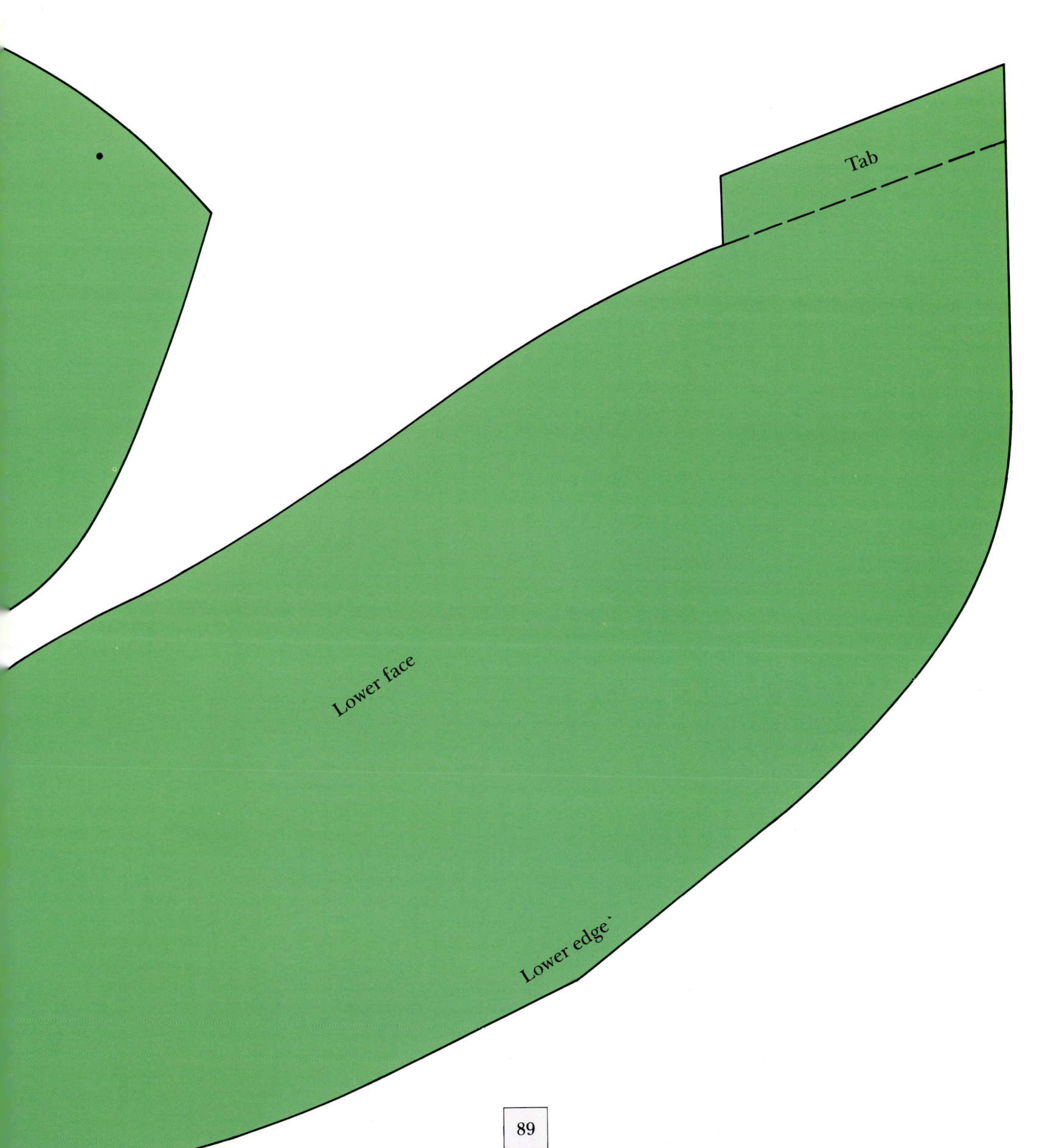

Tab

Lower face

Lower edge

Webbed shoe sole

Webbed shoe upper

Webbed hand

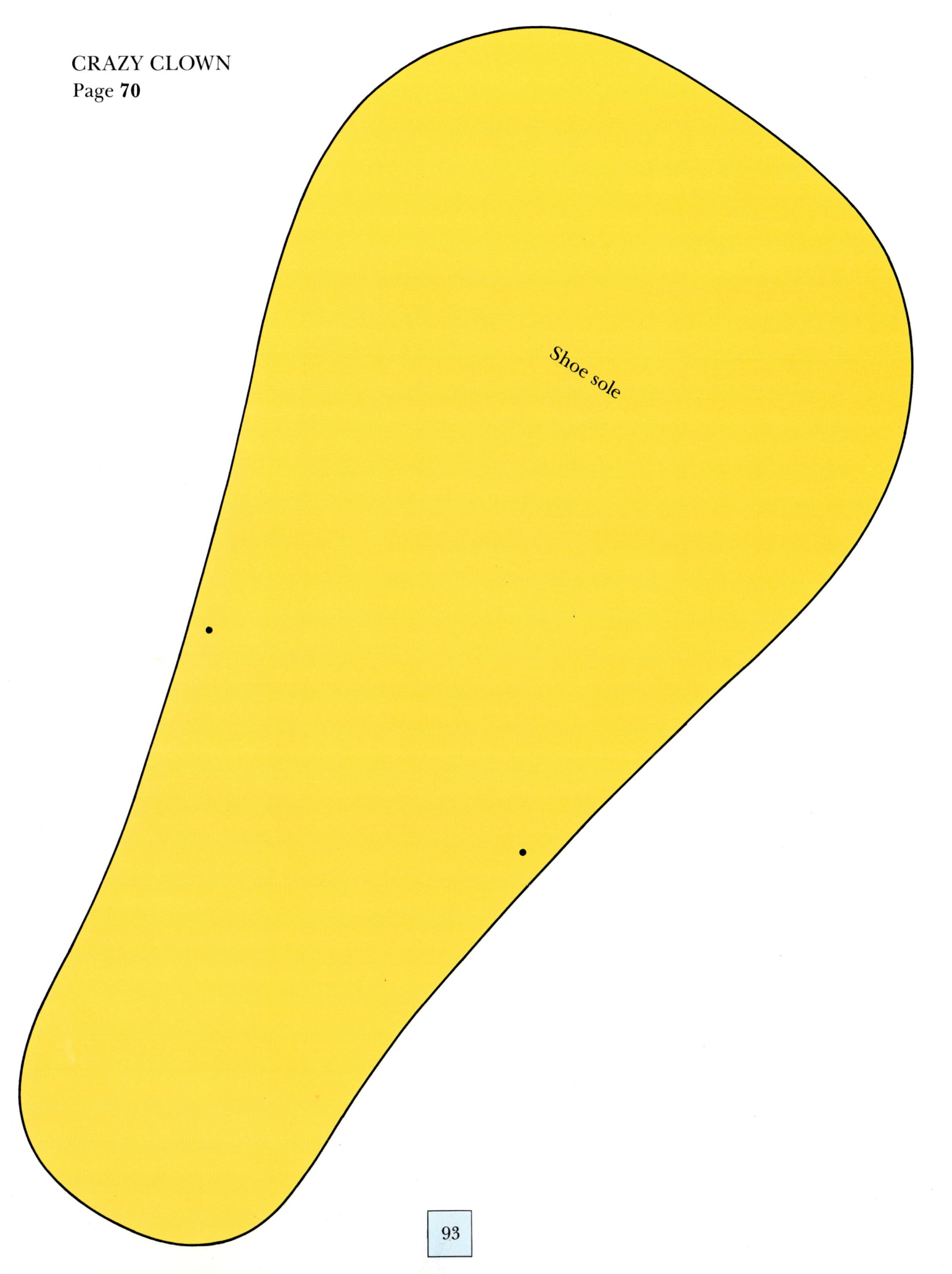

Shoe sole

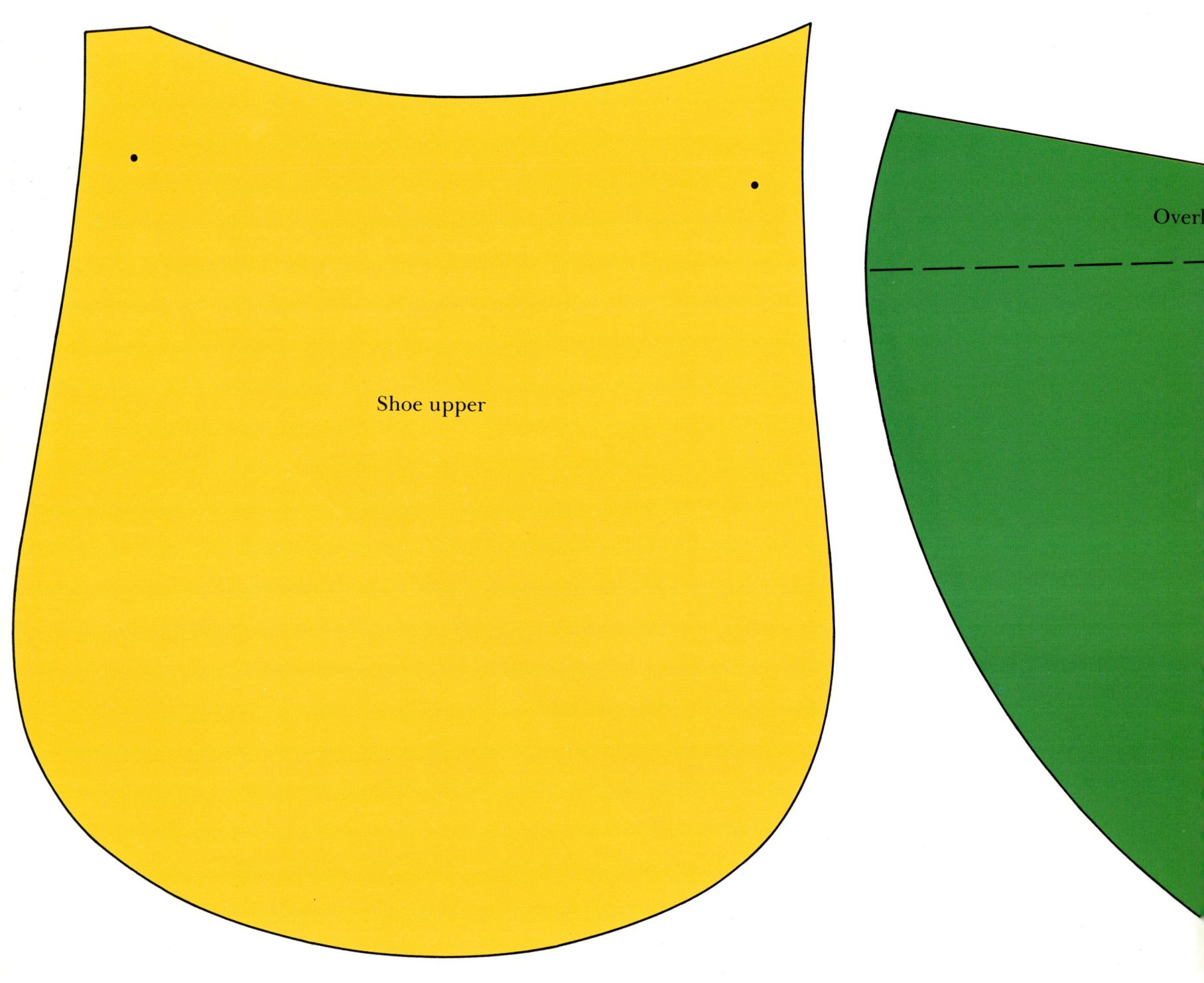

Shoe upper

Overl

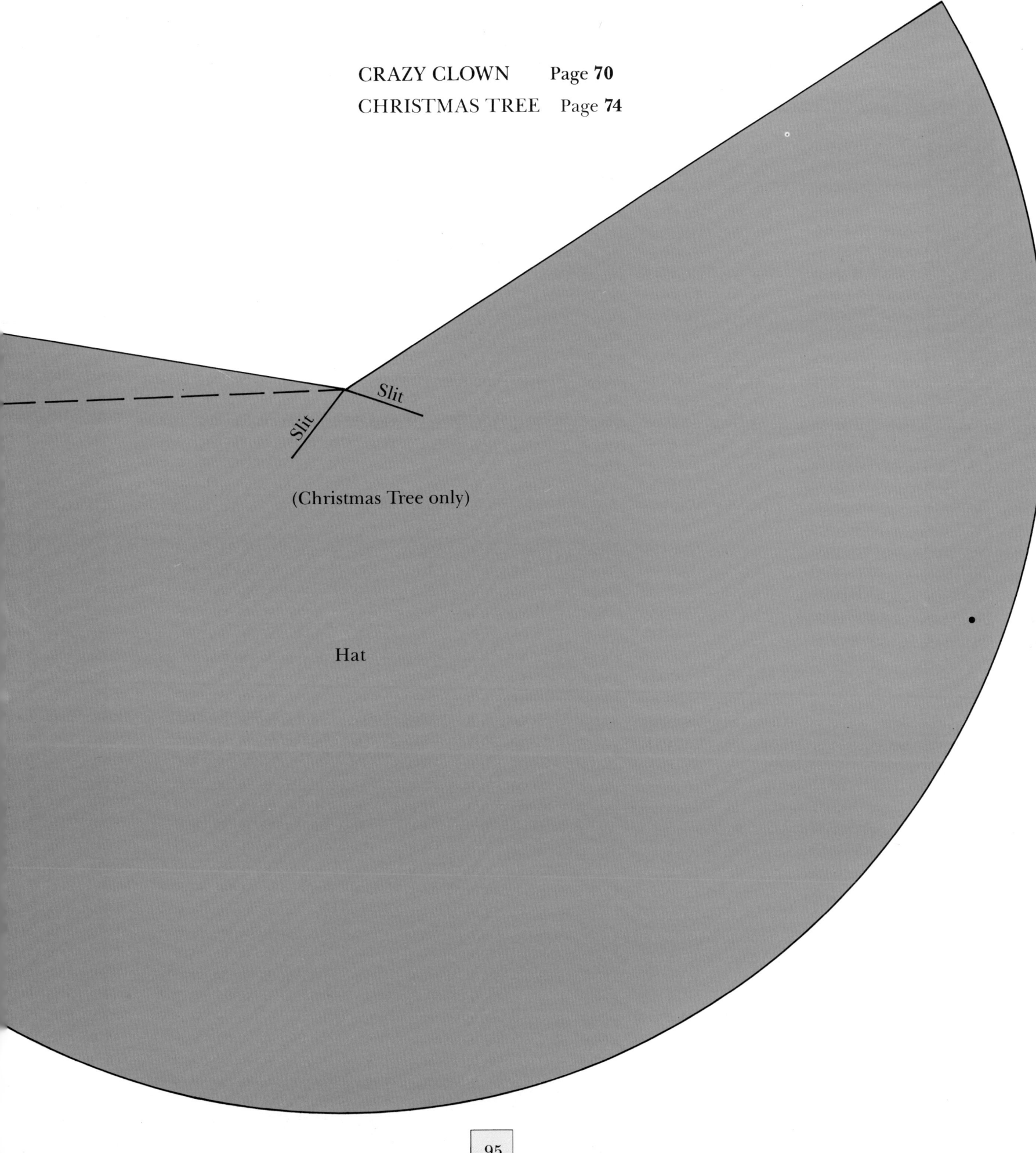

CRAZY CLOWN   Page **70**
CHRISTMAS TREE   Page **74**

Slit

Slit

(Christmas Tree only)

Hat

INDEX

ACKNOWLEDGEMENTS
The author and publishers
would like to thank the
following for their help in
compiling this book:
Hallmark Cards Ltd,
Hallmark House,
Station Road,
Henley-on-Thames,
Oxon RG9 1LQ
(Giftwrap and giftwrapping
ribbons)

Forbo Mayfair,
Station Road,
Cramlington,
Northumberland NE23 8AQ
(Sticky backed plastic)

The Handicraft Shop,
Northgate,
Canterbury,
Kent CT1 1BE
(Craft accessories)

Model Agencies
Kids Plus, 54 Grove Park,
London SE5 8LE
Scallywags, 1 Cranbrook Rise,
Ilford, Essex IG1 3QW
Tiny Tots, 9 Clifton Road,
London W9 1SZ

FURTHER TITLES IN THIS SERIES INCLUDE:

My Craft Book, My Nature Craft Book, My Christmas Craft Book and *My Cookery Book* —
four colourfully illustrated activity books for 7 to 11 year olds. With over thirty-five clever cookery or craft ideas in each book and clear step-by-step instructions to guide the reader, the emphasis is on fun and creativity.

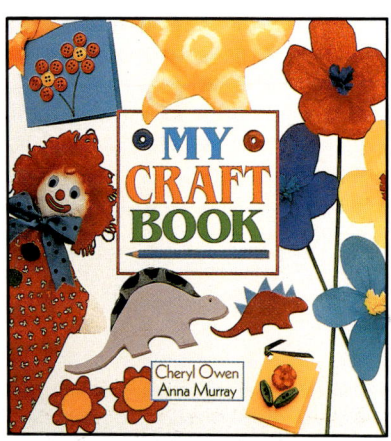
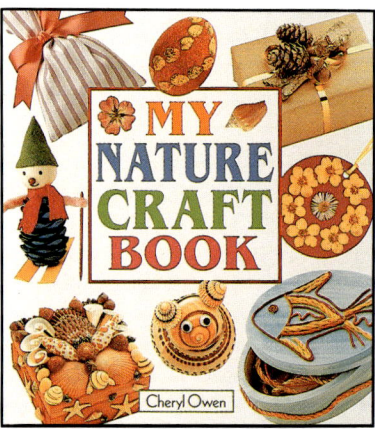